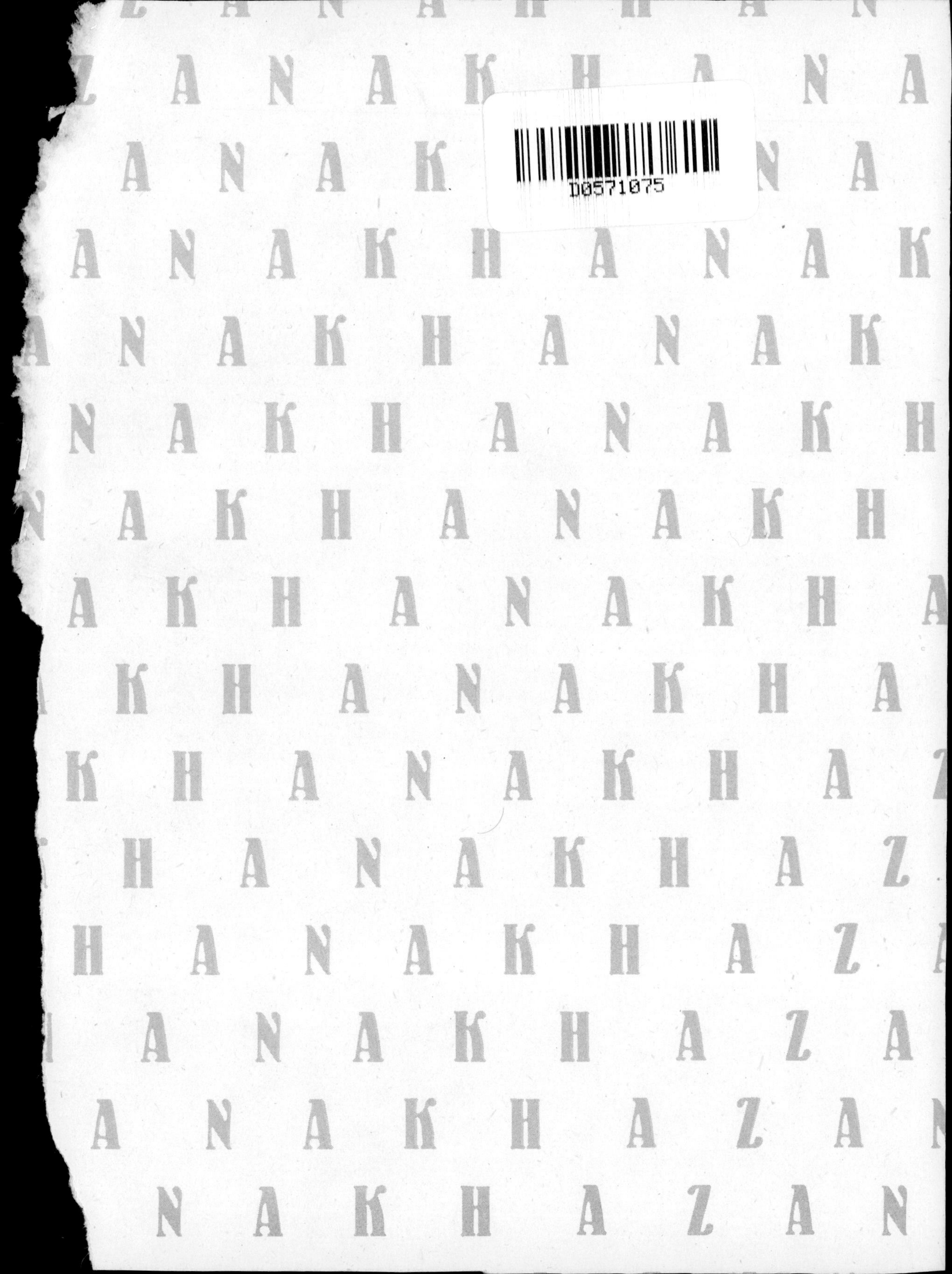

SANJEEV KAPOOR'S

KHANA KHAZANA

CELEBRATION OF INDIAN COOKERY

In association with Alyona Kapoor

Recipes from Tamil Nadu, Kerala, Karnataka and Andhra Pradesh written in association with Chef K. Ganesh.
Recipes from Maharashtra written in association with Milind Sovani, Executive Chef, Centaur, Juhu.

POPULAR PRAKASHAN

POPULAR PRAKASHAN PVT. LTD.
35-C, Pt. Madan Mohan Malaviya Marg
Tardeo, Mumbai-400 034.

First Published 2000
First Reprint August 2000
Second Reprint August 2002
Third Reprint September 2003
Fourth Reprint July 2004
Fifth Reprint February 2006

(3624)

ISBN - 81-7154-680-3

PRINTED IN INDIA
By Saurabh Printers Pvt. Ltd., A-16, Sector-IV,
Noida 201301 and Published by Ramdas Bhatkal
for Popular Prakashan Pvt. Ltd.
35-C, Pt. Madan Mohan Malaviya Marg,
Tardeo, Mumbai-400 034.

This book is dedicated to

my parents

and

all food lovers

who share the same passion that

INDIAN FOOD IS THE BEST

Aashim Malhotra
Anil Bhandari
Anil Jain
Anita & Deepak Chopra
Apurvi Seth
Chef Inder Dev
Chef Manjunath Mural
Chefs of India
Clea PR
Dr. Meena & Ram Prabhoo
Ergotech Studio, Pune
Ganesh Pednekar
Goa Portuguesa Restaurant
Gopi Kukde
Hotel Vallerina, Khandala
Jayakumar
Jijesh Gangadharan
Mr. & Mrs. Kalyanpur
Khazana Restaurant, Dubai
Lohana Khaandaan
National School of Cooking
Neelima Acharya
Nina Murdeshwar
Priyakshi Rajguru Goswami
Puja & Rajeev Kapoor
Rahee Dahake
Rutika Samtani
Sanjiv & Namrata Bahl
Sanjiv Gupta
Satish Parab
Smeeta Bhatkal
Sudipta Majumdar
Sunil Kalia
Pristine Consulting, New Delhi
Vinayak Gawande
Zee Television

Indian Cookery has a vast repertoire of delicacies but unfortunately most of us are not familiar with many of them. This book is the first of a series called *Khana Khazana: Celebration of Indian Cookery* that I have planned in order to familiarize food lovers in India with the cuisine that has been long forgotten. Through this book, I have brought you some easy-to-prepare recipes that will showcase the variety that exists.

Indian Cookery is something that we Indians should take pride in. However, under the guise of progress and modernity we have begun to ape the West and most of us prefer to satisfy our palate with dishes that are foreign to our culture. Interestingly enough, Indian food has become very popular and is available in most parts of the world but it is restricted to a select few dishes. There is an enormous range that has to be yet explored, even by us in India. Each of the states and each region has its own cuisine, which is mostly influenced by the ingredients that are grown locally. But even within a state the food has its own local flavour.

It has taken me a lot of research to fish out recipes which were perfected by our ancestors. Since the recipes come from different parts of India, and have specific names in those languages, they are spelt the way they are pronounced. Every effort has been made to standardize the recipes so that anyone can cook most of the dishes without much ado. As we normally do in our books, we have listed ingredients in their order of usage. The quantities have been mentioned in teaspoons and cups which makes the measurements easy for everybody. Each recipe has been tried and tested by my research team, so that any one who uses the book gets the dish right the first time itself.

Great care has been taken to ensure that the ingredients used are easily available and if not a substitute has been suggested. All recipes serve four and the portion size has been determined by the fact that the dish is a part of a menu where all the dishes complement each other. Chef's tips have been included in recipes where it was felt necessary.

A detailed glossary at the end lists out, in English and Hindi, the various ingredients that are commonly used in Indian cookery. Also listed are some of the utensils that are used widely in India, as also the cooking processes that one should strictly follow in order to get the right results.

All the recipes have been presented in such a way that even a novice would get the desired results, if he/she follows the steps religiously. That Indian cookery is indeed something we should popularize the world over, is a thought that we continue to have faith in. It can be made a universal favourite. All we need to do is start in our own kitchens and spread this art of Indian cooking which has a long tradition. Not a difficult task to achieve. Cook with confidence and share the common belief that Indian food is the best.

Ingredient	Measure	Weight
Almonds	10-12	12 gms
Asafoetida powder (*hing*)	1/2 tspn	5 gms
Baking powder	1 tspn	3 gms
Black gram (*urad*), split	1 cup	220 gms
Black pepper powder	1 tspn	3 gms
Butter	1 tblspn	12 gms
Cashewnuts	10-12	7 gms
Cashewnuts paste	1 cup	140 gms
Chopped coriander leaves	1 cup	55 gms
Cloves	20	1 gms
Coriander (*dhania*) powder	1 tspn	2 gms
	1 tblspn	6 gms
Cumin (*jeera*) powder	1 tspn	2 gms
	1 tblspn	6 gms
Egg	1	63 gms
Flour (*atta*)	1 cup	115 gms
Fresh cream	1 cup	250 mls
	1 tblspn	15 mls
Garam masala powder	1 tspn	2 gms
Garlic	6-8 cloves	5 gms
Garlic paste	1 tblspn	16 gms
Ghee	1 tblspn	7 gms
Ginger	1 inch	15-20 gms
Ginger paste	1 tblspn	16 gms
Gramflour (*besan*)	1 tblspn	10 gms
Grated cheese	1 cup	75 gms
Grated coconut	1 cup	175 gms
Green chillies	10	24 gms
	5	11 gms
Green coriander leaves	1 cup	35 gms
Green peas (frozen)	1 cup	110 gms
Honey	1 tblspn	20 gms
Lemon juice	(1/2 lemon) large sized 1 tspn	3 gms
Mawa (*khoya*)	1 cup	200 gms
Medium sized carrot	1	60 gms
Medium sized onion	1	90 gms
Medium sized potato	1	100 gms
Medium sized tomato	1	100 gms
Mustard (*rai*) powder	1 tspn	2 gms
Oil	1 tblspn	13 mls
Pigeon Pea, split (*toor dal*)	1 cup	225 gms
Red chilli (*mirch*) powder	1 tspn	2 gms
	1 tblspn	5 gms
Refined flour (*maida*)	1 tbslpn	8 gms
	1 cup	200 gms
Rice	1 cup	200 gms
Rice flour	1 tspn	3 gms
	1 tblspn	7 gms
	1 cup	115 gms
Salt	1 tspn	6 gms
Sugar	1 tblspn	14 gms
Tamarind pulp	1 tspn	6 gms
	1 tblspn	16 gms
Turmeric (*haldi*) powder	1 tspn	2 gms
	1 tblspn	7 gms
Vinegar	1 tblspn	11 gms
White pepper	55-60	3 gms
Yogurt	1 tblspn	15 gms

SNACKS, STARTERS AND SOUPS

FISH AND SEAFOOD

CHICKEN

MUTTON

VEGETABLES

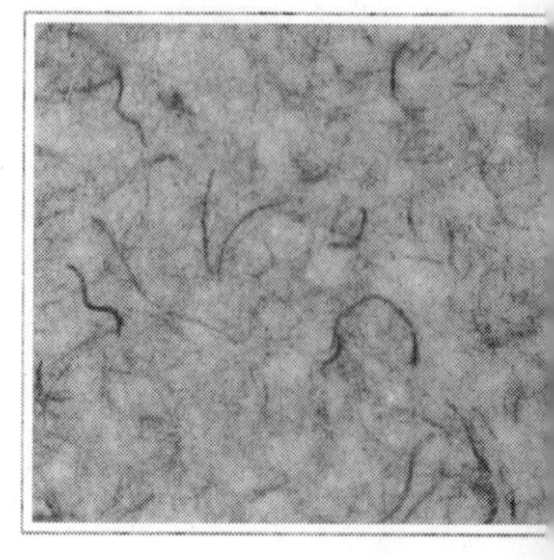

ACCOMPANIMENTS

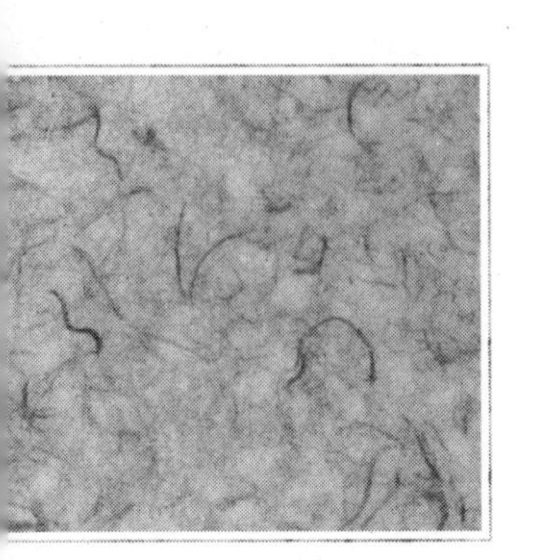

SWEETS

INGREDIENTS

Chicken bones	500 gms	Salt	to taste
Onion	1 medium sized	Turmeric powder	½ tspn
Garlic	4-6 cloves	Red chilli powder	1 tspn
Tamarind	½ lemon sized ball	Asafoetida powder	¼ tspn
Tomato	1 medium sized	Gram flour (*Besan*)	2 tblspns
Curry leaves	16-20	Fresh coconut, scraped	½ cup
Boneless chicken	125 gms	Lemon juice	1 tblspn

METHOD OF PREPARATION

1. Clean and wash chicken bones. Peel and roughly chop onion and garlic.
2. Soak tamarind in quarter cup warm water; remove the pulp, strain and reserve. Wash and roughly chop the tomato and curry leaves.
3. Boil the chicken bones in about seven to eight cups of water, skim the scum from the surface and simmer for ten minutes.
4. Add roughly chopped onion, garlic, tamarind pulp, tomatoes, boneless chicken, salt, turmeric powder, red chilli powder, asafoetida powder and chopped curry leaves. Continue to simmer on medium heat for another fifteen minutes. Remove cooked boneless chicken, cool and chop into bite sized pieces.
5. Blend *besan* in quarter cup water and mix into the simmering soup. Add scraped coconut, cover and simmer for ten to twelve minutes.
6. Strain soup, pressing the residue well to extract the entire flavour.
7. Reheat the soup, add chopped chicken, adjust the seasoning, mix in lemon juice and serve piping hot.

2

INGREDIENTS

Fish fillets	4 medium sized	Salt	to taste
Ginger	1 one inch piece	Rice flour	1 tblspn
Garlic	4-6 cloves	Refined flour	1 tblspn
Green capsicum	2 medium sized	Gram flour (*Besan*)	½ cup
Red chilli powder	1 tblspn	Cooking soda	¼ tspn
Lemon juice	2 tblspns	Oil	for deep-frying

METHOD OF PREPARATION

1. Clean, trim and cut fish into fingers of approximately 2½ x ½ x ½ inches each.
2. Peel ginger and garlic; grind to a fine paste.
3. Wash, halve, remove seeds and cut capsicum lengthwise into half inch broad strips.
4. Mix ginger-garlic paste, red chilli powder, lemon juice and salt to a thick paste. Apply this spice paste uniformly on the fish fingers and the capsicum strips.
5. Mix rice flour, refined flour, gram flour, a little salt and cooking soda thoroughly. Add sufficient water to make a smooth batter of coating consistency. Ensure that no lumps are formed.
6. Take a piece of fish finger, sandwich between two strips of capsicum and secure with two wooden toothpicks.
7. Heat oil in a *kadai*, dip the prepared fish and capsicum in the batter, shake off the excess batter and slide into the hot oil. Deep-fry on medium heat for two to three minutes, turning over frequently or until golden brown and crisp.
8. Drain and keep on an absorbent kitchen towel or paper. Serve hot with coconut *chutney* or tomato ketchup.

INGREDIENTS

Potatoes	4 medium sized	Fresh coriander leaves	¼ cup
Tomatoes	4 medium sized	Green peas, shelled	¼ cup
Cauliflower	¼ small sized	Lemon	2
Onions	2 medium sized	Oil	3 tblspns
Ginger	1 one inch piece	*Pav bhajee masala*	1 ½ tblspns
Garlic	8-10 cloves	Salt	to taste
Capsicum	1 medium sized	Butter	3 tblspns
Green chillies	3-4	*Pav*	8

METHOD OF PREPARATION

1. Boil, cool, peel and grate potatoes. Wash and finely chop tomatoes.
2. Wash and grate cauliflower. Peel and finely chop onions. Peel ginger and garlic; grind to a fine paste. Wash, halve, remove seeds and finely chop capsicum.
3. Wash, remove stems and finely chop green chillies. Clean, wash and finely chop fresh coriander leaves. Boil green peas in salted water till soft, drain, mash lightly and keep aside. Cut lemon into wedges.
4. Heat oil in a pan and add three fourth quantity of chopped onions. Sauté till light brown. Add chopped green chillies and ginger-garlic paste. Stir-fry for half a minute.
5. Add half the quantity of chopped tomatoes and cook on medium heat for three to four minutes, stirring continuously or till oil separates from the *masala*.
6. Add chopped capsicum, boiled and lightly mashed peas, grated cauliflower, grated boiled potatoes and one and half cups water. Bring it to a boil and simmer for ten minutes, pressing with the back of a spoon a few times, till all the vegetables are completely mashed.
7. Add *pav bhajee masala*, salt and rest of the chopped tomatoes. Cook on medium heat for two minutes, stirring continuously.
8. Heat half of the butter in a thick-bottomed pan or a *tawa*. Slice *pav* horizontally into two and pan-fry in butter for half a minute, pressing two or three times or till *pav* is crisp and light brown.
9. Garnish the *bhajee* with chopped coriander leaves, remaining butter and serve hot with *pav* accompanied with remaining chopped onions and lemon wedges.

SENAI ROAST

PAN ROASTED YAM

INGREDIENTS

Yam .... 750 gms
Turmeric powder .... ½ tspn
Semolina (*Rava*) .... 1 cup
Oil .... ½ cup

Masala paste
Dry whole red chillies 8
Cumin seeds .... 1 tspn
Fennel seeds .... 1 tblspn
Tamarind .... 1 lemon sized ball
Peppercorns .... ½ tspn
Curry leaves 10-12
Chana dal .... 1 tblspn
Rice .... 1 tblspn
Salt .... to taste

METHOD OF PREPARATION

1. Peel and cut yam into fingers of approximately 3 x ½ x ½ inches size.
2. Cook yam in salted boiling water with turmeric powder till half cooked and drain. Cool and pat dry the yam fingers on an absorbent kitchen towel.
3. Dry roast the *masala* ingredients including tamarind on a *tawa*. Cool and grind to a smooth and thick paste, adding a little water.
4. Apply the *masala* paste on the yam and refrigerate for about half an hour.
5. Roll the *masala*-coated yam in the semolina, shake off the excess semolina and keep ready.
6. Heat oil in a shallow frying pan, and gently slide the yam fingers in small batches and pan roast over low heat for eight to ten minutes or till it is crisp and golden brown. Roll it continuously for even cooking.
7. Drain on an absorbent kitchen towel or paper and serve hot with your favourite dip.

Chef's Tip: *Try this with potatoes or even sweet potatoes. Breadfruit (Neer Fanas) prepared in this manner also tastes delicious.*

INGREDIENTS

Semolina (*Rava*)	1½ cups
Carrot	1 medium sized
Beans	6-8
Capsicum	1 medium sized
Cauliflower	1 medium sized
Onion	1 medium sized
Ginger	1 inch piece
Green chillies	4
Green peas	¼ cup
Oil	5 tblspns
Mustard seeds	½ tspn
Dry whole red chillies	2
Urad dal	2 tspns
Curry leaves	10-12
Asafoetida powder	¼ tspn
Salt	to taste
Lemon juice	1 tblspn

METHOD OF PREPARATION

1. Roast the semolina in a dry *kadai* without browning, remove and cool. Wash, peel carrot, string beans and cut into small dices. Halve capsicum, remove seeds and cut into small dices. Wash and cut cauliflower into small florets.
2. Peel and chop onion and ginger finely. Wash, remove stems and finely chop green chillies.
3. Boil sufficient water in a pan, add a little salt and boil carrot, beans, cauliflower and green peas for six to eight minutes or till the vegetables are almost done. Drain and reserve the vegetables.
4. Heat oil in a *kadai,* add mustard seeds, stir-fry till they crackle. Add red chillies, *urad dal*, curry leaves and green chillies.
5. Mix well and add the chopped onion, ginger and diced capsicum and continue to cook on high flame for two minutes. Add the cooked vegetables, sprinkle asafoetida powder and salt to taste.
6. Pour four to five cups of hot water and bring to boil. Add roasted semolina, stirring continuously to prevent lump formation.
7. Cook for three to four minutes on medium heat, stirring continuously. Stir in lemon juice and serve hot.

INGREDIENTS

Fresh coriander leaves	4 cups	Cooking soda	a pinch
Green chillies	4	Turmeric powder	½ tspn
Jaggery, grated	2 tspns	Gram flour (*Besan*)	1 cup
Salt	to taste	Oil	2 tblspns + for deep-frying

METHOD OF PREPARATION

1. Clean, wash and finely chop fresh coriander leaves. Reserve two tablespoons for garnish. Wash, remove stems and finely chop green chillies.
2. Combine chopped fresh coriander leaves, green chillies, jaggery, salt, cooking soda, turmeric powder, gram flour and two tablespoons oil. Add enough water to make a thick batter. Ensure that the consistency is not too thin.
3. Pour the batter in a greased plate that is at least one and half inches deep or a tray measuring approximately 6x6x1½ inches.
4. Steam on high heat for fifteen to twenty minutes or till firm and cooked. Check by inserting a skewer into the *wadi* and if it comes out clean, then it is cooked. Remove, cool and cut into one inch sized cubes.
5. Heat sufficient oil in a *kadai* and deep-fry the *wadis* till they are light golden brown in colour and crisp. Drain and keep on an absorbent kitchen towel.
6. Serve hot, garnished liberally with chopped coriander leaves.

INGREDIENTS

Apples	2 medium sized	Capsicum	1 medium sized
Lemon juice	2 tblspns	Spring onions	2 bulbs
Green grapes, seedless	12-15	Fresh coriander leaves	½ cup
Black grapes, seedless	12-15	Fresh mint leaves	a few sprigs
Oranges	2 medium sized	Green chillies	2
Cucumber	1 medium sized	Salt	to taste
Tomatoes	2 medium sized	*Chaat masala*	1 tspn

METHOD OF PREPARATION

1. Wash and core the apples, cut into halves and slice to make thin pieces. Apply one tablespoon lemon juice immediately to prevent discolouration.
2. Wash green and black grapes and cut them into two. Peel oranges and separate the segments. Remove seeds and halve each of them.
3. Peel cucumber, cut into half lengthwise and slice into thin pieces. Wash and cut the tomatoes into two. Remove and discard seeds and cut into thin strips.
4. Wash and cut the capsicum into two. Remove and discard seeds and cut into thin strips. Peel, wash, halve spring onions and cut into thin slices.
5. Clean, wash and finely chop fresh coriander and mint leaves. Wash, remove stems and finely chop green chillies. Mix chopped fresh coriander leaves, mint leaves, green chillies, salt, *chaat masala* and the remaining lemon juice to make a dressing.
6. Toss the prepared fruits in the dressing and serve chilled.

INGREDIENTS

Onion	1 medium sized	Oil	7 tblspns
Salt	to taste	*Bhajanee* flour	3 cups
Turmeric powder	½ tspn		

METHOD OF PREPARATION

1. Peel and finely chop onion.
2. Add salt, turmeric powder, chopped onion and two teaspoons of oil to the *bhajanee* flour. Add water as required, a little at a time and knead to form a soft dough.
3. Divide dough into eight equal portions. Flatten each portion on a moist banana leaf or a thick polythene sheet, into quarter inch thick discs of four to five inches diameter.
4. Make a hole in the centre of each *thalipeeth*. Heat a *tawa,* apply a little oil and transfer *thalipeeth* carefully to the *tawa*. Spoon a little oil on the sides and cook on low flame for one minute.
5. Turn the *thalipeeth* and cook the other side for one minute or till crisp and golden brown.
6. Serve hot with a blob of butter or yogurt.

Chef's Tip: *To make bhajanee flour, dry roast the ingredients, listed below, separately. Cool, mix and grind to a fine powder. It can be stored upto one month.*

Whole wheat	1 cup	Black *chana*	¾ cup
Rice	1 cup	*Urad dal*	¾ cup
Jawar	2 cups	Coriander seeds	½ cup
Bajra	2 cups		

Kothimbir Wadi, Bhajanee Thalipeeth

Mulayam Murgh Seekh

INGREDIENTS

Fresh coriander leaves .... ¼ cup
Green chillies 2-3
Ginger .... 1 one inch piece
Garlic .... 4-6 cloves
Cashewnuts 8-10
Minced chicken, from the breast .... ½ kg
Egg yolks 2
Salt .... to taste
Garam masala powder .... 1 tspn
White pepper powder .... 1 tspn
Butter .... 2 tblspns
Lemon juice .... 1 tblspn
Chaat masala .... 1 tspn

METHOD OF PREPARATION

1. Clean, wash and finely chop fresh coriander leaves. Wash, remove stems and roughly chop green chillies. Peel ginger and garlic; grind with chopped fresh coriander and green chillies to a fine paste without adding water.
2. Soak cashewnuts in warm water for ten minutes, drain and grind to a fine paste.
3. Blend ginger, garlic, coriander and green chilli paste with cashewnut paste and egg yolks. Mix this with chicken mince and add salt, *garam masala* powder and white pepper powder. Mix thoroughly and keep aside, preferably in the refrigerator for at least half an hour.
4. Divide the prepared chicken mixture into ten to twelve equal sized portions. Moisten your palms and spread each portion on to a skewer and shape them into *kababs* of four to five inches length.
5. Cook in a moderately hot *tandoor* for about eight to ten minutes turning them occasionally.
6. Brush the cooked *kababs* with butter and cook again for a minute in the *tandoor.*
7. They can also be cooked in a preheated oven at 220 degrees Celsius for about ten minutes. Brush the *kababs* with butter and cook for two minutes more.
8. Sprinkle lemon juice and *chaat masala* on the cooked *kababs* and serve hot.

INGREDIENTS

Sweet potatoes	6-8 medium sized	Cumin seeds	1 tspn
Onion	1 medium sized	Black salt, powdered	1 tspn
Garlic	3-4 cloves	Salt	to taste
Green chillies	2	Lemon juice	2 tblspns
Fresh coriander leaves	¼ cup	Black peppercorns, crushed	½ tspn
Mint leaves	¼ cup		

METHOD OF PREPARATION

1. Wash and boil sweet potatoes in sufficient water till completely cooked. Cool, peel and cut into bite sized pieces.
2. Peel and finely chop onion. Peel and roughly chop garlic. Wash, remove stems and roughly chop green chillies.
3. Clean, wash and finely chop fresh coriander and mint leaves. Dry roast cumin seeds and grind to a fine powder.
4. Mix fresh coriander leaves, mint leaves, garlic and green chillies and grind to a fine paste.
5. Mix together cooked sweet potato pieces, ground paste, roasted cumin powder, black salt powder, salt, lemon juice, chopped onions and crushed black peppercorns. Toss well and serve at room temperature.

INGREDIENTS

Ingredient	Quantity
Carrots	3 medium sized
Red pumpkin	500 gms
Onion	1 medium sized
Green chillies	2
Cumin seeds	1 tspn
Fresh coriander leaves	a few sprigs
Salt	to taste
Fresh orange juice	1 cup
Fresh cream	½ cup

METHOD OF PREPARATION

1. Wash, peel and roughly chop carrots. Peel, remove seeds of the red pumpkin and roughly chop into pieces. Peel and roughly chop onion. Wash, remove stems and chop green chillies.
2. Dry roast cumin seeds, cool and grind to a fine powder. Clean, wash and pat dry fresh coriander leaves.
3. Heat a saucepan; add chopped carrots, red pumpkin, onion, green chillies and one cup water. Cook on medium heat for eight to ten minutes or till the vegetables are soft.
4. Cool the cooked vegetables slightly and make a puree in the blender.
5. Add roasted cumin powder, salt and one cup water to the vegetable puree and bring to a boil. Reduce heat, add fresh orange juice and simmer for two to three minutes.
6. Stir in fresh cream and serve hot, garnished with fresh coriander leaves.

DAHI SHORBA

TEMPERED YOGURT SOUP

INGREDIENTS

Ingredient	Quantity
Carrot	1 medium sized
French beans	4-6
Capsicum	1 medium sized
Cauliflower	5-6 small florets
Green chillies	1-2
Ginger	1 one inch piece
Yogurt	1 cup
Gram flour *(Besan)*	2 tspns
Sugar	¼ tspn
Salt	to taste
Pure *ghee*	2 tspns
Cumin seeds	1 tspn
Green peas, shelled	2 tblspns

METHOD OF PREPARATION

1. Wash, peel and finely chop carrot. Wash, string and finely chop French beans. Wash, halve, remove seeds and finely chop capsicum. Wash and finely chop the cauliflower florets.
2. Wash, remove stems and roughly chop green chillies. Peel ginger and grind with chopped green chillies to a fine paste.
3. Whisk yogurt with three cups water. Add gram flour, ginger-chilli paste, sugar and salt to the yogurt and blend well.
4. Heat *ghee* in a thick-bottomed vessel, add cumin seeds and stir-fry until light brown. Add chopped carrot, beans, capsicum, green peas and cauliflower. Stir well and sauté vegetables for two to three minutes.
5. Stir in the yogurt mixture, bring to a boil, reduce heat and simmer for eight to ten minutes or until it thickens to a soup consistency.
6. Adjust seasoning and serve hot.

INGREDIENTS

Toor dal .... 4 tblspns
Fresh coriander leaves .... ¼ cup
Tamarind .... ½ lemon sized ball
Tomatoes .... 2 medium sized
Dry whole red chillies 2
Rasam powder .... 1½ tspns
Asafoetida powder .... ¼ tspn
Salt .... to taste
Curry leaves 10-12
Pure *ghee* .... 4 tblspns
Mustard seeds .... ½ tspn

METHOD OF PREPARATION

1. Wash, drain and cook *toor dal* in two cups of water until soft. Strain and mash cooked *dal* well. Reserve the strained cooking liquor. Clean, wash and finely chop fresh coriander leaves. Reserve two tablespoons chopped coriander leaves for garnish.
2. Soak tamarind in one cup warm water; remove pulp, strain and reserve. Wash and chop tomatoes. Remove stems and break red chillies into two.
3. Mix tamarind pulp with chopped coriander leaves, *rasam* powder, asafoetida powder, salt and half the quantity of curry leaves and bring to a boil. Reduce heat and simmer for two to three minutes.
4. Add chopped tomatoes and the reserved cooking liquor. Simmer for four to five minutes and add mashed *dal*. Stir well and cook for a minute more.
5. Remove from fire and sprinkle the reserved chopped coriander leaves.
6. Heat pure *ghee* in a tempering pan, add mustard seeds and stir-fry till they crackle. Add broken red chillies and remaining curry leaves and stir well. Pour the tempering over the prepared *rasam* and cover immediately to trap the aroma. Serve hot.

Chef's Tip: *You can strain this* rasam *and serve in small tumblers with a lemon wedge, as an appetizer. Traditionally all* rasams *are made in a vessel made from a special alloy. This gives a unique flavour to the preparation.*

LEHSUNI TIKKI

GARLIC FLAVOURED POTATO PATTIES

INGREDIENTS

Potatoes ....6 medium sized
Salt ....to taste
Onion ....1 medium sized
Garlic ....4-6 cloves
Fresh coriander leaves ....¼ cup
Cashewnuts 6-8
Red chilli powder .... ½ tblspn
Paneer, grated .... ¼ cup
Oil ....for deep-frying

METHOD OF PREPARATION

1. Wash and boil the potatoes. Peel and mash them thoroughly. Add salt and knead mashed potatoes to make smooth dough. Divide into ten to twelve equal portions.
2. Peel and finely chop the onion and garlic. Clean, wash and finely chop fresh coriander leaves.
3. Crush cashewnuts and mix with chopped onion, garlic, coriander leaves, red chilli powder, salt, and grated *paneer*. Divide the mixture into ten to twelve equal portions.
4. Stuff each portion of mashed potato with a portion of the *paneer* mixture. Roll and shape into *tikkis* of approximately two inches diameter and half inch thickness.
5. Heat oil in a *kadai* and deep-fry the *tikkis* to golden brown. Remove and drain on a clean and absorbent kitchen towel or paper.
6. Serve hot with tomato ketchup or mint *chutney*.

Chef's Tip: *Typically no binding is used in this recipe. However you could add two to three tablespoons of cornflour to this potato mixture. You may also shallow-fry the tikkis.*

INGREDIENTS

Ingredient	Quantity
Whole *moong* (with skin)	1 cup
Onion	1 medium sized
Ginger	1 one inch piece
Green chillies	4
Black peppercorns	½ tspn
Cumin seeds	½ tspn
Fresh coriander leaves	¼ cup
Curry leaves	10-12
Dry whole red chillies	4
Rice flour	1 tblspn
Salt	to taste
Oil	as required

METHOD OF PREPARATION

1. Clean, wash and soak whole *moong* for about two to three hours. Peel and roughly chop onion and ginger. Wash, remove stems and roughly chop green chillies.
2. Crush peppercorns and cumin seeds. Clean, wash and finely chop the coriander leaves and curry leaves.
3. Drain and grind *moong* along with onion, ginger, green and red chillies.
4. Mix in crushed peppercorns, cumin seeds, chopped coriander leaves, curry leaves, rice flour and salt.
5. Heat a non-stick *tawa* or a *dosa* griddle, brush with a little oil.
6. Spread a ladleful of this batter, to about six inches in diameter with a round spoon to as thin a consistency as possible.
7. Pour a little oil around the edges, cover with a dome type lid and cook for two to three minutes on medium heat. Turn over, pour some more oil and cook the other side for a few minutes or till golden and crisp.
8. Serve hot with *chutney* or *sambhar*.

Chef's Tip: *Traditionally it is made very spicy, but you can reduce the chillies to suit your taste.*

MACHER CHOP

FISH CUTLETS

INGREDIENTS

Fish, preferably *rohu* .... 500 gms
Potatoes .... 2 large sized
Fresh coriander leaves ..... a few sprigs
Green chillies 2-3
Onions .... 2 medium sized
Eggs 2
Oil ...... 2 tblspn + for deep-frying
Raisins .... 1 tblspn
Salt .... to taste
White pepper powder .... ½ tspn
Turmeric powder .... ¼ tspn
Vinegar .... 1 tblspn
Breadcrumbs .... 1 cup

METHOD OF PREPARATION

1. Clean, wash and drain fish. Poach or steam fish on medium heat for three to four minutes. Cool, remove skin, bones and flake fish meat. Boil, cool, peel and mash potatoes.
2. Clean, wash and finely chop fresh coriander leaves. Wash, remove stems and finely chop green chillies
3. Peel and finely chop onions. Whisk the eggs lightly.
4. Heat two tablespoons oil in a pan and add chopped onions and sauté till light golden brown. Remove from heat and add flaked fish, mashed potatoes, chopped fresh coriander leaves, green chillies, raisins, salt, pepper powder, turmeric powder and vinegar.
5. Mix thoroughly and divide into ten to twelve equal portions. Shape into round patties of half inch thickness.
6. Dip the patties in whisked egg; coat with breadcrumbs. Heat oil in a *kadai* and deep-fry fish patties in hot oil till golden brown.
7. Remove from oil, drain on an absorbent kitchen towel and serve hot.

Malwani Prawn Curry

Crab Sukhe

INGREDIENTS

Eggs	8	Gram flour (*Besan*)	3 tblspns
Fresh coriander leaves	½ bunch	*Ajwain*	¼ tspn
Fenugreek leaves (*Methi Saag*)	1 cup	Red chilli powder	½ tspn
Onion	1 large sized	*Chaat masala*	1 tspn
Ginger	2 one inch pieces	Cumin powder	½ tspn
Green chillies	4-5	Cooking soda	¼ tspn
Spring onions	3	Salt	to taste
		Oil	for deep-frying

METHOD OF PREPARATION

1. Boil water and cook eggs for about ten to twelve minutes or till they are hard-boiled. Drain and immediately put into cold water. Remove shells and chop finely.
2. Clean, wash and finely chop fresh coriander and *methi saag*. Peel and finely chop onion and ginger. Wash, remove stems and finely chop green chillies. Wash, trim and finely chop the spring onions, along with the leaves.
3. Mix chopped *methi saag*, fresh coriander leaves, onion, ginger, green chillies and spring onions. Sprinkle *besan* and mix well. Add *ajwain*, red chilli powder, *chaat masala*, cumin powder, cooking soda and salt.
4. Add chopped boiled eggs, sprinkle a little water and mix to combine all the ingredients well.
5. Heat oil in a *kadai*, wet a tablespoon, scoop the egg mixture and gently drop into the hot oil. Fry the *pakoras* in small batches without overcrowding the *kadai*.
6. Cook for two minutes, turning the *pakoras* occasionally for even browning. Transfer the fried *pakoras* to an absorbent kitchen towel or paper.
7. Serve hot with tomato ketchup or green *chutney*.

INGREDIENTS

King fish (*Surmai*) .... 8 half-inch thick slices
Lemon juice .... 4 tblspns
Ginger .... 1 one inch knob
Garlic .... 6-8 cloves
Red chilli powder .... 1 tblspn
Turmeric powder .... 1 tspn
Black pepper, crushed .... ½ tblspn
Gram flour (*Besan*) .... 4 tblspns
Ajwain .... ½ tspn
Salt .... to taste
Mustard oil .... 2 tblspns
Oil .... for frying
Chaat masala .... 2 tspns

METHOD OF PREPARATION

1. Clean, wash and pat dry fish slices. Smear two tablespoons lemon juice and little salt on the fish slices and keep aside.
2. Peel ginger, garlic and grind to a fine paste.
3. Blend ginger-garlic paste with red chilli powder, turmeric powder, crushed black pepper, *besan*, *ajwain*, salt, mustard oil and remaining lemon juice to make a smooth paste.
4. Apply this paste liberally on the fish slices and leave to marinate for half an hour, preferably in the refrigerator.
5. Heat oil in a pan, slide in the marinated fish slices and shallow-fry for two minutes. Turn over and fry for two minutes more or until completely cooked and crisp.
6. Remove and drain on an absorbent kitchen towel or paper and serve hot, liberally sprinkled with *chaat masala*.

Chef's Tip: *Instead of fish slices you can use one inch sized boneless fish chunks.*

INGREDIENTS

King fish (*Surmai*)	8 one inch thick slices
Turmeric powder	1 tspn
Lemon juice	2 tblspns
Salt	to taste
Kodumpuli	4-6
Onion	1 medium sized
Raw mangoes	2 medium sized
Green chillies	4
Fresh coconut, scraped	1 cup
Oil	8 tblspns
Red chilli powder	1 tblspn
Coriander powder	1 tblspn
Rice flour	1½ tblspns
Mustard seeds	½ tspn
Curry leaves	10-12
Dry whole red chillies	2

METHOD OF PREPARATION

1. Clean, wash and pat dry king fish slices. Marinate in a mixture of turmeric powder, lemon juice and salt.
2. Soak *kodumpuli* in half cup warm water for fifteen minutes, mash well and keep aside. Peel and finely chop onion. Wash, peel, remove seeds and cut the raw mangoes into finger sized pieces. Wash, remove stems and slit green chillies.
3. Soak scraped coconut in one cup warm water for three to four minutes. Grind and squeeze to extract thick milk. Reserve the coconut residue for the curry.
4. Heat two tablespoons oil in a frying pan and shallow-fry marinated fish slices on high heat on both sides till golden brown. Remove and keep warm.
5. Heat four tablespoons oil, add chopped onion and cook on high heat for four to five minutes or until it starts turning brown. Add slit green chillies, turmeric powder, red chilli powder and coriander powder.
6. Stir, add soaked *kodumpuli* and simmer for a minute. Add coconut residue and four cups water. Bring to a boil, add rice flour blended in quarter cup water and simmer on medium heat for ten minutes stirring occasionally.
7. Strain curry through a mesh pressing well to extract all the flavours.
8. Heat remaining oil in a pan, add mustard seeds and stir-fry till they start crackling. Add curry leaves and red chillies broken into two.
9. Stir well, add mango pieces and sauté for a minute and pour into the strained curry. Add salt to taste and simmer for two to three minutes. Gently slide in fried fish slices and cook for another two minutes.
10. Remove from heat, add coconut milk and stir well. Reheat on low flame for two to three minutes and serve hot.

Chef's Tip: *Traditionally this curry is made in a clay pot. Tastes excellent with steamed rice, therefore, keep the consistency of the curry a little thin. You can use any kind of fish or seafood and prepare this curry.*

AMBAT TEEKHAT POMFRET

SOUR AND SPICY CURRIED FISH

INGREDIENTS

Pomfret, 300-350 gms each	2-3
Lemon juice	1 tblspn
Salt	to taste
Onions	2 medium sized
Tamarind	1 lemon sized ball
Oil	3 tblspns
Turmeric powder	1 tspn
Coconut milk	½ cup

For masala paste

Garlic	5-6 cloves
Peppercorns	½ tspn
Dry whole red chillies	6-8
Coriander seeds	2 tspns
Fresh coconut, scraped	1 cup

For garnishing

Fresh coriander leaves	¼ cup

METHOD OF PREPARATION

1. Clean, wash and cut fish into one and a half inch thick slices and pat dry on an absorbent kitchen towel. Mix lemon juice with a little salt, apply liberally on the fish slices and keep aside.
2. Peel and finely chop the onions. Clean, wash and chop fresh coriander leaves. Peel garlic.
3. Soak tamarind in one cup of warm water for half an hour, remove pulp, strain and keep aside.
4. Dry roast peppercorns, garlic, red chillies and coriander seeds separately and grind to a paste along with scraped coconut.
5. Heat oil in a pan, add chopped onions and stir-fry for two minutes or till translucent. Add *masala* paste and turmeric powder and sauté for two to three minutes.
6. Add two cups of warm water, tamarind pulp and salt. Bring it to a boil, reduce heat and cook further on medium heat for three to four minutes.
7. Gently slide in the pomfret slices and cook on medium heat for four to five minutes or till the fish is firm and cooked. Stir in coconut milk, reduce heat and simmer for a minute.
8. Garnish with chopped coriander leaves and serve hot, accompanied with steamed rice.

Chef's Tip: *You can replace pomfret with any other fish or seafood in this recipe.*

INGREDIENTS

Pomfret	2 large sized	Green chillies	2
Coconut toddy vinegar	2 tblspns	Curry leaves	8-10
Salt	to taste	Oil	4 tblspns
Ginger	1 one inch piece	Mustard seeds	1 tspn
Garlic	3-4 cloves	Turmeric powder	½ tspn
Kodumpuli	6	Red chilli powder	1 tblspn
Onion	1 medium sized	Cumin powder	1 tblspn
Tomato	1 medium sized		

METHOD OF PREPARATION

1. Clean, wash and cut fish into one and a half inch thick slices and pat dry with an absorbent kitchen towel. Mix vinegar with a little salt, apply liberally on the fish slices and keep aside.
2. Peel ginger and garlic; grind to a fine paste. Soak *kodumpuli* in half cup warm water for fifteen minutes, mash well.
3. Peel and finely chop onion. Wash and finely chop tomato. Wash, remove stems, slit green chillies into two and keep. Wash curry leaves and pat dry.
4. Heat oil in a pan, add mustard seeds, stir-fry till they crackle and add curry leaves and green chillies. Add chopped onions and sauté till they start turning golden brown.
5. Add ginger-garlic paste and stir-fry for half a minute. Add turmeric powder, red chilli powder, cumin powder and salt to taste.
6. Stir well and add chopped tomatoes and *kodumpuli* alongwith the water and simmer for five minutes. Add marinated fish slices and one and half cups water.
7. Stir, bring to a boil, and cover with a tight-fitting lid. Reduce heat and simmer for eight to ten minutes or till the fish is tender and flaky.
8. Serve hot with steamed rice.

Chef's Tip: *The fish head can be used to get full flavour and aroma in the curry. Traditionally this dish is prepared in an earthen pot.*

INGREDIENTS

Fish, preferably *rohu*	1 small sized
Salt	to taste
Turmeric powder	2 tspns
Potatoes	2 medium sized
Green chillies	5
Coriander seeds	1 ½ tblspns
Cumin seeds	1 tspn
Mustard oil	3 tblspns
Nigella seeds (*Kalonji*)	¼ tspn

METHOD OF PREPARATION

1. Clean, cut and remove the head of the fish. Clean the insides of the fish and wash thoroughly. Cut the fish into half inch thick slices. Pat dry with a kitchen towel and apply salt and turmeric powder.
2. Wash, peel and cut potatoes into half inch thick finger sized pieces. Wash, remove stems and slit the green chillies. Dry roast coriander and cumin seeds briefly, cool and grind to a fine paste, adding a little water.
3. Heat two tablespoons of mustard oil in a pan till it reaches smoking point. Remove, cool and heat the oil again on medium heat. Add the fish slices, a few at a time, and fry for a minute on each side. Drain and keep aside.
4. Add potato pieces to the pan and sauté for two to three minutes. Heat remaining oil in the same pan, add *kalonji,* slit green chillies and stir-fry briefly.
5. Add coriander-cumin paste and cook on low heat for a minute sprinkling a little water if required.
6. Add two cups of water, sautéed potatoes and salt; simmer for four to five minutes or until the potatoes are completely cooked.
7. Gently slide in the pan-fried fish slices and simmer for two to three minutes or until the fish is cooked. Serve hot with steamed rice.

INGREDIENTS

Prawns, shelled .... 12-16 medium sized	Ginger .... 1 one inch piece
Salt .... to taste	Bay leaves 2
Turmeric powder .... ½ tspn	Green cardamoms 3-4
Oil .... 2 tblspns	Cloves 3-4
Onions .... 2 medium sized	Cinnamon .... 1 one inch stick
Fresh coconut, scraped .... 1 ½ cups	Red chilli powder .... 1 tspn
	Pure *ghee* .... 1 tblspn

METHOD OF PREPARATION

1. Clean, devein and wash the prawns thoroughly. Apply a little salt and turmeric powder.
2. Heat half tablespoon oil in a pan and sauté the prawns on medium heat for two to three minutes. Remove from heat and keep aside.
3. Peel and grate the onions. Reserve one tablespoon scraped coconut and grind the remaining with one and a half cups warm water. Squeeze and extract coconut milk. Peel ginger and grind to a fine paste.
4. Heat remaining oil in a pan; add bay leaves, green cardamoms, cloves and cinnamon. Stir-fry briefly. Add grated onions and sauté for two to three minutes or until the onions turn translucent.
5. Blend the red chilli powder in a little water and add to the onions. Stir-fry on medium heat for two to three minutes or until oil separates. Add ginger paste and continue to cook for about two minutes sprinkling little water from time to time to prevent burning.
6. Add the sautéed prawns and coconut milk. Simmer for two minutes, mix in pure *ghee,* salt and the reserved scraped coconut and serve hot.

INGREDIENTS

Prawns, shelled	12-16 medium sized	Red chilli powder	2 tblspns
Ginger	1 one inch piece	Turmeric powder	½ tspn
Garlic	6-8 cloves	Salt	to taste
Cumin powder	1 tspn	Rice flour	2 tblspns
Tamarind pulp	1 tblspn	Oil	¼ cup
		Lemon juice	1 tblspn

METHOD OF PREPARATION

1. Devein, wash and pat dry prawns with a clean kitchen towel. Peel ginger and garlic; grind to a fine paste.
2. Mix ginger-garlic paste with cumin powder, tamarind pulp, red chilli powder, turmeric powder, salt and rice flour and blend two tablespoons oil in this mixture.
3. Marinate prawns in this mixture and leave aside for at least two hours, preferably in the refrigerator.
4. Heat oil in a pan, add the marinated prawns and cook for a minute on high heat. Turn over the prawns and cook for another minute. Reduce heat and cook for two to three minutes turning the prawns occasionally for uniform cooking.
5. Remove, drain on an absorbent kitchen towel or paper, sprinkle lemon juice on the cooked prawns and serve hot.

Prawn Varuval

Fried Bangda

INGREDIENTS

Whole mackerel (*Bangda*) .... 8 medium sized
Salt .... to taste
Lemon juice .... 2 tblspns
Ginger .... 2 one inch pieces
Garlic .... 12-15 cloves
Kokam 10-12
Red chilli powder .... 3 tspns
Turmeric powder .... ½ tspn
Oil .... for shallow-frying
Rice powder, coarse .... 1 cup

For garnishing

Lemon 1

METHOD OF PREPARATION

1. Make a small slit at the stomach and clean the insides of the mackerel and wash thoroughly. Make four to five quarter inch deep cuts on both the sides, apply salt and lemon juice. Keep aside for fifteen minutes.
2. Peel ginger, garlic and grind to a fine paste. Soak *kokam* in half a cup of warm water for fifteen minutes, remove the pulp, strain and keep aside.
3. Mix red chilli powder, turmeric powder, ginger-garlic paste, *kokam* pulp, and salt and marinate mackerels in this paste for half an hour, preferably in a refrigerator.
4. Heat oil in a frying pan. Roll the fish in rice powder and shallow-fry the fish in small batches, without overcrowding the pan, for two to three minutes.
5. Turn the fish and continue to cook on medium heat for two minutes or till the mackerel is light brown and crisp.
6. Serve hot garnished with lemon wedges.

CHUTNEY FISH

FISH COOKED IN MINT AND RAW MANGO CHUTNEY

INGREDIENTS

Betki fillets .... 600 gms
Salt .... to taste
Lemon juice .... 2 tblspns
Spinach .... ½ medium sized bundle
Mint leaves .... ½ cup
Fresh coriander leaves .... ½ cup
Green chillies 4
Onion .... 1 large sized
Ginger .... 1 one inch piece
Garlic .... 4-5 cloves
Raw mango .... 1 small sized
Oil .... 6 tblspns
Coriander powder .... 2 tblspns
Cumin powder .... 1 tspn
Fresh cream .... 2 tblspns

METHOD OF PREPARATION

1. Clean, wash and cut fish fillets into one and a half inch sized pieces. Apply salt and lemon juice and keep aside.
2. Clean, wash and roughly chop spinach, mint and fresh coriander leaves. Wash, remove stems and finely chop green chillies. Peel and finely chop onion, ginger and garlic. Peel, remove seed and roughly chop raw mango.
3. Grind mint leaves, fresh coriander leaves and green chillies and raw mango to a fine paste, adding a little water.
4. Heat four tablespoons oil and shallow-fry fish pieces for two to three minutes, turning them gently, to a light brown colour. Keep aside the cooked fish on an absorbent kitchen towel or paper.
5. Heat the remaining oil in a pan, add chopped onion and sauté for two to three minutes on medium heat or until they are translucent. Add chopped ginger and garlic and stir-fry briefly.
6. Add coriander powder, cumin powder and stir well. Add chopped spinach and cook for two minutes on medium heat, stirring continuously.
7. Stir in the mint, coriander, green chilli and raw mango paste, add one cup water and salt to taste and bring to a boil. Reduce heat and simmer for two to three minutes, stirring occasionally.
8. Gently slide in the shallow-fried fish pieces, stir gently and simmer for two minutes more.
9. Stir in the fresh cream and serve hot.

INGREDIENTS

Lobsters	4 medium sized	Red chilli powder	2 tspns
Yogurt	1 cup	Cumin powder	2 tspns
Ginger	1 one inch piece	Turmeric powder	½ tspn
Garlic	5-6 cloves	Gram flour (*Besan*)	2 tblspns
Egg yolk	1	Lemon juice	2 tblspns
Fresh cream	2 tblspns	Salt	to taste
Ajwain	2 tspns	Butter	2 tblspns
White pepper powder	½ tspn	*Chaat Masala*	½ tspn

METHOD OF PREPARATION

1. Remove shells, clean and devein the lobsters, then wash them thoroughly. Tie the yogurt in a muslin cloth and hang it for half an hour to drain out the whey. This should preferably be hung in the refrigerator.
2. Peel ginger, garlic and grind to a fine paste.
3. Transfer the hung yogurt to a bowl, add egg yolk and whisk well to blend.
4. Add ginger-garlic paste, fresh cream, *ajwain*, white pepper powder, red chilli powder, cumin powder, turmeric powder, *besan*, lemon juice and salt.
5. Mix well and coat the lobsters uniformly with the yogurt mixture. Keep aside to marinate, preferably in the refrigerator, for two to three hours.
6. Skewer the marinated lobsters and cook in a moderately hot *tandoor* for about five to six minutes, turning them occasionally.
7. Brush the cooked lobsters with butter and cook again for a minute in the *tandoor.*
8. They can also be cooked in a preheated oven at 200 degrees Celsius for about six to eight minutes. Brush the lobsters with butter and cook for a minute more.
9. Sprinkle *chaat masala* on the cooked lobsters and serve hot with lemon wedges and mint *chutney*.

CRAB SUKHE

CRAB MASALA

INGREDIENTS

Crabs	4 (approx. 150-200 gms each)
Onions	3 medium sized
Ginger	1 one inch piece
Garlic	12-16 cloves
Fresh coriander leaves	a few sprigs
Tamarind	1 lemon sized ball
Oil	4 tblspns
Fresh coconut, scraped	1½ cups
Mustard seeds	½ tspn
Curry leaves	6-7
Turmeric powder	½ tspn
Malwani masala	1 tspn
Red chilli powder	1 tspn
Salt	to taste

METHOD OF PREPARATION

1. Clean crabs and wash thoroughly. Detach and crack the claws. Cut each into two pieces. Peel and finely slice onions and ginger.
2. Peel garlic. Clean, wash and finely chop fresh coriander leaves. Soak tamarind in one cup warm water for half an hour, remove the pulp, strain and keep aside.
3. Heat one tablespoon oil in a pan and pan-roast sliced onions, sliced ginger, scraped coconut and garlic till light golden brown.
4. Remove from heat and cool. Add a little water and grind to a thick paste.
5. Heat remaining oil in a pan, add mustard seeds and when they start crackling add curry leaves. Add *masala* paste, cook on medium heat for half a minute, stirring continuously.
6. Add turmeric powder, dry *Malwani masala*, red chilli powder, tamarind pulp and salt. Stir well and add one cup of water. Bring it to a boil and add crab pieces and claws.
7. Cook further on medium heat for ten to fifteen minutes, stirring continuously or till the gravy becomes a little thick.
8. Serve hot, garnished with fresh coriander leaves.

INGREDIENTS

Prawns, shelled	16 medium sized
Salt	to taste
Onions	3 medium sized
Garlic	6 cloves
Fresh coriander leaves	a few sprigs
Oil	3 tblspns
Kokam	5-6 pieces
Coconut milk	½ cup
For paste	
Onion	1 large
Garlic	6 cloves
Dry whole red chillies	8
Fresh coconut, scraped	1 cup
Coriander seeds	2 tspns
Turmeric powder	¼ tspn

METHOD OF PREPARATION

1. Devein, wash, drain prawns and apply half teaspoon salt to them. Peel and finely chop onions and garlic. Clean, wash and finely chop coriander leaves.
2. For the paste peel and finely chop onions and garlic. Soak red chillies in half a cup of warm water.
3. Reserve one tablespoon of scraped coconut and dry roast the remaining coconut and chopped onions for the paste in a thick-bottomed *kadai* over medium heat for two to three minutes, stirring continuously or till coconut turns light golden brown in colour.
4. Cool the roasted coconut and onion mixture and grind to a paste along with coriander seeds, turmeric powder, garlic and soaked red chillies. Marinate prawns in this paste and keep aside until required.
5. Heat oil in a pan, add chopped onions and garlic. Cook on medium heat, stirring continuously till light golden brown.
6. Add the marinated prawns, *kokam* and one cup of water. Bring it to a boil and add salt. Reduce heat and simmer for two minutes. Stir in coconut milk and continue to simmer for two more minutes, taking care not to overcook the prawns.
7. Serve hot, garnished with reserved scraped coconut and chopped coriander leaves.

CHETTINAAD FRIED CHICKEN

DRY AND SPICY PAN-FRIED CHICKEN

INGREDIENTS

Chicken	1 medium sized	Turmeric powder	½ tspn
Onions	2 medium sized	Lemon juice	1 tblspn
Ginger	1 one inch piece	Rice flour	2 tblspns
Garlic	4-6 cloves	Salt	to taste
Green chillies	4	Curry leaves	10-12
Dry whole red chillies	4-6	Oil	to shallow fry

METHOD OF PREPARATION

1. Clean, wash and slit chicken through the backbone and the breast, into two equal halves. Make three to four half inch deep cuts on breast and leg pieces.
2. Peel and roughly chop onions, ginger and garlic, and grind to a smooth paste along with green and red chillies, adding a little water if required. Wash, drain and finely shred curry leaves.
3. Blend turmeric powder, lemon juice and rice flour into the *masala* paste and mix in salt to taste.
4. Apply this mixture thoroughly and liberally on the chicken and leave to marinate for two to three hours, preferably in the refrigerator. Mix in shredded curry leaves into the chicken.
5. Heat oil in a shallow pan, add marinated chicken and sauté for two minutes on both sides to seal the exterior.
6. Reduce heat to medium, cover with a lid and cook for fifteen to twenty minutes, turning over and basting frequently with the remaining marinade. Sprinkle a little water if the chicken starts drying.
7. The last few minutes of the cooking should be done on high heat, so that the surface of the chicken is crisp and golden brown.
8. Cut into smaller pieces and serve hot.

INGREDIENTS

Chicken	1 medium sized	Cinnamon	1 inch stick
Onions	4 medium sized	Green cardamoms	3-4
Ginger	1 inch piece	Cloves	3-4
Garlic	3-4 cloves	Star anise	1
Green chillies	2	Bay leaves	2
Turmeric powder	½ tspn	Red chilli powder	1 tblspn
Lemon juice	1½ tblspns	Coriander powder	1½ tblspns
Salt	to taste	Mustard seeds	½ tspn
Fresh coconut, scraped	1 cup	Curry leaves	10-12
Oil	6 tblspns	Dry whole red chillies	2

METHOD OF PREPARATION

1. Wash, clean and cut chicken into ten to twelve equal sized pieces.
2. Peel and finely chop onions. Peel ginger and garlic; grind to a smooth paste with green chillies.
3. Marinate chicken in turmeric powder, ginger-garlic and green chilli paste, lemon juice and salt. Leave aside to marinate for about half an hour, preferably in the refrigerator.
4. Grind scraped coconut with one cup warm water, extract thick milk, and repeat once again with two cups water to get a second extract and keep.
5. Heat four tablespoons oil in a thick-bottomed pan, add whole spices and stir-fry briefly. Add chopped onions and sauté till they start to turn light brown. Add red chilli powder and coriander powder and mix.
6. Add chicken pieces, sauté for a few minutes to seal the exterior, pour the second coconut extract, cover and cook on medium heat for ten to fifteen minutes or till the chicken is cooked.
7. Remove from fire, add first extract of coconut milk and reheat on medium flame for three to four minutes, stirring occasionally.
8. Heat remaining oil, stir in mustard seeds and when they start crackling, add curry leaves and red chillies. Pour the tempering into the prepared chicken curry and immediately cover to trap the flavour and aroma.
9. Adjust seasoning and serve hot.

ANDHRA CHILLI CHICKEN

FIERY PAN-FRIED CHILLI CHICKEN

INGREDIENTS

Chicken	1 medium sized	Dry whole red chillies	8-10
Salt	to taste	Rice	2 tblspns
Lemon juice	4 tblspns	Yogurt	½ cup
Ginger	2 one inch pieces	Fresh coriander leaves	½ cup
Garlic	6-8 cloves	Oil	¼ cup
Curry leaves	8-10	Refined flour	¼ cup

METHOD OF PREPARATION

1. Clean, wash and cut the chicken into four — two leg pieces and two breast pieces. Make four to five half inch deep slits on the pieces. Apply salt and two tablespoons lemon juice and keep aside.
2. Peel ginger and garlic; grind with curry leaves, red chillies and rice to a smooth paste by adding the remaining lemon juice. Blend this paste into the yogurt and whisk well to a smooth consistency. Add salt to taste.
3. Apply this yogurt mixture liberally on the chicken pieces and leave to marinate for four to six hours, preferably in the refrigerator. Clean, wash and finely chop fresh coriander leaves.
4. Heat oil in a pan, roll the marinated chicken pieces in refined flour, shake the excess flour and shallow-fry. Cook for one minute, turn over the chicken pieces and cook for another minute.
5. Reduce heat and cook for five to six minutes, turning the chicken pieces frequently for uniform cooking. Remove and drain the chicken.
6. Transfer the chicken to a shallow pan and keep on medium heat. Sprinkle chopped coriander leaves and two tablespoons water; cover with a fitting lid. Reduce heat and cook for five minutes on low heat or until the chicken is completely cooked.
7. Serve hot.

Andhra Chilli Chicken

Pistewala Murgh

INGREDIENTS

- Chicken, boneless .... 500 gms
- Onions .... 2 large sized
- Ginger .... 1 one inch piece
- Garlic .... 4-5 cloves
- Yogurt .... ½ cup
- Pistachio nuts .... ½ cup
- Green chillies 4
- Oil .... 4 tblspns
- Coriander powder .... 2 tblspns
- White pepper powder .... ½ tspn
- Salt .... to taste
- Fresh cream .... ½ cup
- *Garam masala* powder .... ½ tspn

METHOD OF PREPARATION

1. Wash, trim and cut the chicken into one and a half inch sized pieces.
2. Peel, quarter and boil onions in one cup water. Drain, cool lightly and grind to a fine paste. Peel ginger and garlic and grind to a fine paste. Whisk yogurt and keep aside.
3. Soak pistachio nuts in hot water for ten minutes, drain and peel. Wash, remove stems and finely chop green chillies. Reserve a few peeled pistachio nuts for garnish.
4. Grind the remaining peeled pistachio nuts with chopped green chillies to a fine paste, adding a little water.
5. Heat oil in a pan, add boiled onion paste and sauté for three to four minutes or until the oil starts oozing out. Ensure that the colour of the onions does not change to brown.
6. Add ginger-garlic paste and stir-fry briefly. Add coriander powder, white pepper powder and salt; mix well. Stir in the pistachio and green chillies paste and cook for a minute.
7. Add chicken pieces and sauté for two minutes. Reduce heat, add one cup water and simmer for four to five minutes or until the chicken is completely cooked. Stir in yogurt and continue to simmer for two minutes, stirring occasionally.
8. Stir in fresh cream, sprinkle *garam masala* powder, remaining pistachio nuts and serve hot.

INGREDIENTS

Chicken, skinless	1 medium sized	Onions	5 medium sized
Coconut, dry	½	Dry whole red chillies	4-5
Fresh coriander leaves	¼ cup	Oil	4 tblspns
Green chillies	2-3	Fresh coconut, scraped	1½ cups
Ginger	1 one inch piece	*Malwani garam masala*	2 ½ tspns
Garlic	4-5 cloves	Salt	to taste

METHOD OF PREPARATION

1. Wash, clean and cut chicken into sixteen pieces. Grate dry coconut.
2. Clean, wash and roughly chop fresh coriander leaves. Wash green chillies, remove the stems and chop roughly. Peel and chop ginger and garlic roughly. Peel onions and finely chop.
3. Reserve one tablespoon of fresh coriander leaves for garnish. Grind remaining fresh coriander leaves to a paste along with garlic, ginger and green chillies and marinate the chicken in this paste.
4. Dry roast grated dry coconut with red chillies and make a fine paste by adding a little water.
5. Heat one tablespoon oil in a pan, add three-fourth quantity of chopped onions, stir-fry till golden. Add fresh coconut; continue to cook on medium heat, stirring continuously till coconut changes its colour to light brown. Cool and grind to a fine paste, adding a little water.
6. Heat remaining oil in a *handi,* add remaining chopped onions and stir-fry till golden brown. Add the green paste coated chicken pieces and two cups of water and bring it to a boil.
7. Stir in dry coconut and red chilli paste and *Malwani garam masala*. Continue to cook for three to four minutes on medium heat.
8. Add the fresh coconut and onion paste and cook further on medium heat for three to four minutes. Add salt and mix thoroughly.
9. Garnish with chopped fresh coriander leaves. Serve with *Malwani wada* which is a special rice flour *puri.*

INGREDIENTS

Chicken, skinless .... 1 medium sized (approx. 1 kg)
Onions .... 3 medium sized
Ginger .... 1 one inch piece
Garlic .... 6-8 cloves
Fresh coriander leaves .... a few sprigs
Oil .... 5 tblspns
Dry whole red chillies 3-4
Turmeric powder .... ¼ tspn
Nutmeg, grated .... a pinch
Kolhapuri dry *chutney* .... 1 tspn
Salt .... to taste

For paste

Dry coconut .... ¼
Bedgi red chillies 8-10
Sesame seeds .... 1 tblspn
Poppy seeds .... 2 tblspns
Peppercorns 6-8
Shahi jeera .... 1 tspn
Cinnamon .... 1 one inch stick
Green cardamoms 3-4
Black cardamom 1
Cloves 4-5
Mace .... 1 blade

METHOD OF PREPARATION

1. Clean, wash and cut chicken, into twelve to fourteen pieces.
2. Peel and finely chop onions. Peel ginger, garlic and grind to a fine paste. Clean, wash and finely chop fresh coriander leaves.
3. Grate dry coconut. Clean and remove stems from *bedgi* red chillies. Dry roast sesame seeds, poppy seeds, peppercorns, *shahi jeera*, cinnamon, green cardamoms, black cardamoms, cloves and mace separately.
4. Cool and grind all roasted spices along with dry coconut and *bedgi* red chillies to a fine paste, adding a little water.
5. Heat oil in a thick-bottomed pan, add cleaned red chillies, stir-fry briefly, remove and reserve for garnish. Add chopped onions to the same oil and sauté till golden brown.
6. Add ginger-garlic paste and cook on medium heat for a few seconds.
7. Stir in the coconut paste and cook further for three to four minutes on medium heat, stirring frequently.
8. Add chicken pieces, mix well and cook on high heat, stirring continuously, for two to three minutes.
9. Add half a cup of water and continue cooking on medium heat for three to four minutes, stirring frequently.
10. Add turmeric powder, grated nutmeg, *Kolhapuri* dry *chutney* and salt. Mix well and cook further till chicken is completely cooked, stirring frequently.
11. The *masala* should be quite thick and dry. Serve hot garnished with chopped fresh coriander leaves and fried red chillies.

MURGH CHAANDI KORMA

NIZAMI CHICKEN PREPARATION

INGREDIENTS

Chicken, skinless	1 medium sized	Oil	¼ cup
Onions	3 medium sized	*Khoya*, grated	½ cup
Green chillies	3-4	White pepper powder	1 tspn
Ginger	1 one inch piece	Salt	to taste
Garlic	6-8 cloves	Fresh cream	¼ cup
Almonds	10-12	Green cardamom powder	½ tspn
Pistachio nuts	6-8	Dried rose petals	8-10
Yogurt	1 cup	Silver *varq*	for garnish

METHOD OF PREPARATION

1. Clean, wash and cut chicken into twelve to fifteen pieces.
2. Peel and finely chop onions. Wash, remove stems and roughly chop green chillies. Peel ginger and garlic and grind to a fine paste along with chopped green chillies.
3. Soak almonds and pistachio nuts in one cup warm water for ten minutes, drain and peel. Reserve three to four almonds for garnish and grind the remaining to a fine paste. Slice the reserved almonds and pistachio nuts.
4. Whisk yogurt with half cup water till smooth.
5. Heat oil in a deep pan, add sliced onions and sauté till it turns light golden brown.
6. Add the ginger, garlic and green chilli paste and stir-fry for two minutes.
7. Stir in the almond paste, grated *khoya* and one cup warm water. Reduce heat and cook for ten to fifteen minutes, stirring frequently.
8. Add chicken pieces and whisked yogurt. Cook covered on medium heat for eight to ten minutes, stirring occasionally.
9. Add white pepper powder and salt. Stir well and simmer for three to four minutes more or until the chicken is completely cooked.
10. Add fresh cream, cardamom powder and lightly crushed rose petals. Stir well and simmer for two minutes.
11. Garnish with silver *varq*, almond and pistachio slices and serve hot.

Chef's Tip: *In case you want the chicken to be spicier, you can add more green chillies and white pepper powder.*

INGREDIENTS

Onions	3 medium sized
Tomatoes	2 medium sized
Ginger	1 one inch piece
Garlic	8-10 cloves
Green peas, shelled	½ cup
Salt	to taste
Fresh coriander leaves	a few sprigs
Oil	3 tblspns
Green cardamoms	3-4
Black cardamoms	1
Cloves	3-4
Cinnamon	2 one inch sticks
Bay leaves	2
Mutton mince	½ kg
Red chilli powder	1½ tspns
Turmeric powder	¼ tspn
Cumin powder	1 tspn
Coriander powder	1 tblspn
Garam masala powder	1 tspn
Butter	2 tblspns
Pav or bread rolls	8

METHOD OF PREPARATION

1. Peel and finely chop onions. Wash and finely chop tomatoes. Peel ginger and garlic; grind to a fine paste.
2. Boil green peas in salted boiling water for five minutes or till almost cooked. Refresh in cold water. Drain and leave aside.
3. Clean, wash and finely chop fresh coriander leaves.
4. Heat oil in a thick-bottomed pan, add green and black cardamoms, cloves, cinnamon and bay leaves. Stir-fry briefly.
5. Add chopped onions and cook on medium heat, till they turn golden brown, stirring continuously. Add ginger and garlic paste and stir briefly. Add chopped tomatoes and cook till oil starts separating from the *masala*.
6. Add mutton mince and cook on high heat for three to four minutes, stirring continuously. Reduce heat, stir in half a cup of water and cook covered till mince is completely cooked. Stir occasionally.
7. Add red chilli powder, turmeric powder, cumin powder, coriander powder, salt and boiled green peas. Mix well and cook on high heat for a couple of minutes or till the mince is quite dry.
8. Sprinkle *garam masala* powder and garnish with chopped coriander leaves.
9. Heat butter in a thick-bottomed pan or a *tawa*. Slice *pav* horizontally into two and pan-fry in butter for half a minute, pressing two or three times or till *pav* is crisp and light brown.
10. Serve mince accompanied with pan-fried *pavs*.

MUTTON ISHTEW

MUTTON AND POTATO STEWED IN COCONUT MILK

INGREDIENTS

Mutton, preferably from leg	750 gms
Potatoes	2 medium sized
Green chillies	4-5
Fresh coconut, scraped	2 cups
Peppercorns	½ tspn
Cumin seeds	¼ tspn
Chana dal	2 tspns
Coriander seeds	½ tspn
Oil	4 tblspns
Star anise	2
Cinnamon	1 one inch stick
Green cardamoms	4
Curry leaves	10-12
Salt	to taste

METHOD OF PREPARATION

1. Clean, wash and cut mutton into one and a half inch sized pieces and pat dry. Wash, peel potatoes and cut them into six to eight medium sized pieces. Wash, remove stems and slit green chillies.
2. Soak scraped coconut in two cups warm water, grind to extract milk and keep. Repeat this process two more times but with only one cup water to get a second and third extract.
3. Dry roast peppercorns, cumin seeds, *chana dal* and coriander seeds on medium heat, cool and grind to a powder.
4. Pressure cook mutton in two cups water until almost done, drain and keep aside.
5. Heat oil in a thick-bottomed pan, add star anise, cinnamon, green cardamoms and stir-fry briefly. Add pressure-cooked mutton, potato pieces, curry leaves and slit green chillies. Sprinkle powdered *masala* and cook, stirring continuously.
6. Add third coconut extract, bring to a boil, reduce heat and cook on medium heat for ten to twelve minutes or till potatoes are almost cooked. Add second extract and continue cooking till both the mutton and potatoes are completely cooked.
7. Remove from fire and stir in first extract of coconut milk and salt to taste. Reheat and simmer for two to three minutes before serving hot with *aappams* or *porottas*.

Chef's Tip: *Instead of throwing the water in which the mutton has been cooked, use it as a stock for meat based soups.*

INGREDIENTS

Mutton .... 600 gms
Salt .... to taste
Dry apricots (*Jardalu*) 6-8
Onions .... 2 medium sized
Ginger .... 2 one inch pieces
Garlic .... 6-8 cloves
Dry whole red chillies 4
Cumin seeds .... 1 tblspn
Tomato .... 1 medium sized
Potatoes .... 2 medium sized
Oil .... 2 tblspns + for deep frying
Red chilli powder .... 1 tspn
Turmeric powder .... ½ tspn
Worcestershire sauce (optional) .... 2 tblspns
Jaggery, grated .... 2 tspns
Vinegar .... 2 tblspns

METHOD OF PREPARATION

1. Clean, wash and cut the mutton into one and a half inch sized pieces. Rub salt into the mutton pieces and keep aside. Soak dry apricots in one cup hot water for fifteen minutes.
2. Peel and finely chop onions. Peel ginger and garlic and grind with red chillies and cumin seeds to a fine paste, adding a little water. Wash and finely chop tomato.
3. Peel, thinly slice and shred the potatoes into matchstick sized pieces. Soak the potato pieces in water for ten minutes, drain and pat dry.
4. Heat oil in a *kadai* and deep-fry potato matchsticks in hot oil till crisp and golden brown. Drain and transfer to an absorbent kitchen towel or paper.
5. Heat oil in a pan and sauté chopped onions until they turn light golden brown. Add ginger, garlic, red chilli and cumin paste, red chilli powder and turmeric powder and stir-fry briefly.
6. Add mutton pieces and sauté for two to three minutes. Stir in two cups water and the apricots, along with the water they were soaked in and bring to a boil.
7. Reduce heat, cover and simmer for fifteen to twenty minutes or until the mutton is completely cooked. Add chopped tomatoes and cook on high heat for two to three minutes, stirring continuously.
8. Add salt and stir in Worcestershire sauce, jaggery and vinegar. Transfer the mutton to a serving dish, garnish liberally with the fried potato pieces and serve hot.

MUTTON URUNDAI KOZHAMBU

MINCED MUTTON BALLS IN TAMARIND CURRY

INGREDIENTS

- Mutton mince ... 450 gms
- Mutton fat ... 2 tblspns
- Eggs ... 2
- Onions ... 2 medium sized
- Tomatoes ... 2 medium sized
- Tamarind ... 1 lemon sized ball
- Fresh coriander leaves ... ¼ cup
- Turmeric powder ... 1 tspn
- Salt ... to taste
- Oil ... 8 tblspns

Masala paste

- Poppy seeds ... 2 tspns
- Ginger ... 1 one inch piece
- Garlic ... 4-5 cloves
- Green chillies ... 4
- Fresh coconut, scraped ... ¼ cup

Masala powder

- Dry whole red chillies ... 2
- Peppercorns ... 1 tblspn
- *Chana dal* ... 2 tblspns
- Coriander seeds ... 2 tblspns
- Cinnamon ... 1 one inch stick
- Cloves ... 2
- Star anise ... 1
- Cardamoms ... 2
- Nutmeg, grated ... ¼ tspn

METHOD OF PREPARATION

1. Clean mutton mince and pound mutton fat into it till well blended. Mix in eggs with light hands.
2. Peel and finely chop onions. Wash and puree tomatoes in a blender. Soak tamarind in two cups warm water; remove pulp and strain.
3. Soak poppy seeds in two tablespoons warm water. Peel ginger and garlic and roughly chop. Wash, remove stems and roughly chop green chillies. Grind chopped ginger, garlic and green chillies with soaked poppy seeds and scraped coconut to a fine paste.
4. Clean, wash and finely chop coriander leaves and keep some aside for garnishing.
5. Dry roast the *masala* powder ingredients, cool and grind to a coarse powder.
6. Mix in chopped coriander leaves, turmeric powder, salt and a quarter part of the *masala* paste and the *masala* powder into the mutton mince and keep aside for at least an hour to marinate, preferably in the refrigerator.
7. Divide mince into sixteen equal parts, wet your palm and form into smooth balls. Cover with a wet cloth and keep.
8. Heat oil in a wide-mouthed shallow pan, add onions and sauté till golden brown. Add remaining *masala* paste and continue to cook.
9. Pour in tomato puree, tamarind pulp and one cup water. Cook on medium heat for five to six minutes or till the fat separates.
10. Add remaining *masala* powder and simmer for a minute. Add a little more water if required.
11. Gently slide in mutton balls and cook on low heat for fifteen minutes or till the mutton balls are cooked.
12. Serve hot garnished with the reserved coriander leaves.

Mutton Urandai Kozhambu

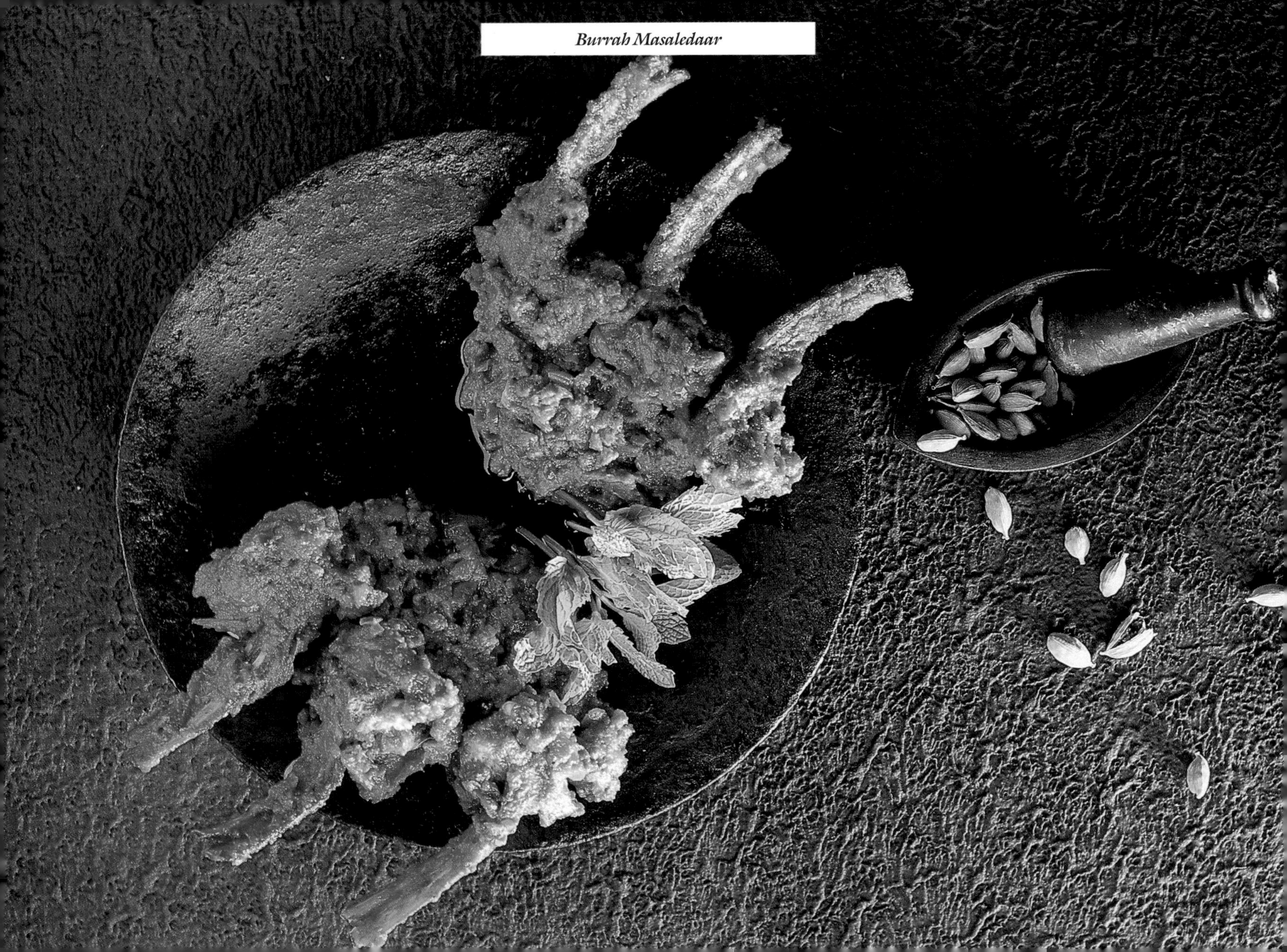

Burrah Masaledaar

INGREDIENTS

Lamb chops	12-15
Onions	2 medium sized
Tomatoes	2 medium sized
Ginger	2 one inch pieces
Garlic	6-8 cloves
Raw papaya	2 one inch pieces
Yogurt	1 cup
Fresh coriander leaves	a few sprigs
Coriander seeds	1 tblspn
Cumin seeds	1½ tspns
Cloves	4-6
Black cardamoms	2
Mace	1 blade
Peppercorns	1 tspn
Dry whole red chillies	2
Salt	to taste
Oil	¼ cup
Kashmiri red chilli powder	1½ tspns

METHOD OF PREPARATION

1. Clean, wash and pat dry lamb chops. Peel and finely chop onions. Wash and finely chop tomatoes. Peel ginger and garlic; grind to a fine paste. Peel and grind raw papaya to a fine paste. Alternately grate raw papaya.
2. Tie the yogurt in a muslin cloth and hang it for half an hour to drain out the whey. This should preferably be hung in the refrigerator.
3. Clean, wash and finely chop fresh coriander leaves. Dry roast coriander seeds, cumin seeds, cloves, black cardamoms, mace, peppercorns and red chillies. Cool and powder.
4. Transfer the hung yogurt to a bowl and mix in the raw papaya paste and salt. Marinate the lamb chops in this mixture for about two hours.
5. Heat oil in a pan, add the chopped onions and sauté for three to four minutes or until they turn light golden brown. Add ginger-garlic paste and stir-fry briefly.
6. Mix in the prepared spice powder, Kashmiri red chilli powder and cook on medium heat for two minutes.
7. Add the marinated lamb chops along with the marinade and one cup water and bring to a boil.
8. Reduce heat, cover and cook for fifteen to twenty minutes or till the mutton chops are completely cooked.
9. Add chopped tomatoes and cook on high heat for four to five minutes, stirring frequently. Ensure that the gravy is quite thick.
10. Garnish with chopped fresh coriander leaves and serve hot.

52

KOLHAPURI PANDHARA RASSA

SPICED MUTTON GRAVY

INGREDIENTS

Fresh coriander leaves	a few sprigs
Onions	2 medium sized
Ginger	1 one inch piece
Garlic	6-8 cloves
Oil	4 tblspns
Nutmeg, grated	a pinch
Cinnamon	1 one inch stick
Green cardamoms	4-5
Black cardamoms	2-3
Cloves	5-6
Mace	1 blade
Bay leaves	2
Mutton stock	5 cups
Salt	to taste
White pepper powder	2 tspns
For paste	
Sesame seeds	1 tblspn
Poppy seeds	2 tblspns
Fresh coconut, scraped	¾ cup

METHOD OF PREPARATION

1. Dry roast sesame seeds in a pan. Soak poppy seeds in quarter cup water for fifteen to twenty minutes.
2. Boil sesame seeds and poppy seeds together in half a cup of water and let it cool. Drain and grind sesame seeds, poppy seeds and scraped coconut to a fine paste, adding a little water, if required.
3. Clean, wash and finely chop fresh coriander leaves. Peel, cut into quarters and boil onions in one cup water for three to four minutes. Drain, cool and grind to a fine paste. Peel ginger and garlic, grind to a fine paste.
4. Heat oil in a thick-bottomed pan, add nutmeg, cinnamon, green cardamoms, black cardamoms, cloves, mace and bay leaves. Stir-fry briefly.
5. Add boiled onion paste, cook on medium heat for five to six minutes stirring continuously. Ensure that most of the moisture evaporates but do not brown the onion paste.
6. Add ginger-garlic paste, cook further on medium heat for a few seconds.
7. Add sesame, poppy and coconut paste and continue to cook on medium heat for three to four minutes, stirring continuously.
8. Add mutton stock, bring it to a boil. Reduce heat and simmer for three to four minutes. Add salt, white pepper powder dissolved in quarter cup water and mix well.
9. Simmer for another ten to fifteen minutes and serve hot garnished with fresh coriander leaves.

***Chef's Tip:** Mutton stock can be prepared by boiling half a kilogram of mutton with bones with one and a half litres of water till mutton is cooked. Use the stock for* pandhara rassa *and mutton pieces to make other mutton dishes. In Kolhapur, apart from* pandhara rassa *(white mutton gravy)*, tambada rassa *(red mutton gravy) is also equally popular.*

INGREDIENTS

Spinach	4 medium sized bundles
Garlic	12-15 cloves
Green chillies	4
Rice flour	1 tblspn
Tamarind	½ lemon sized ball
Dry whole red chillies	3-4
Curry leaves	10-12
Til oil	4 tblspns
Mustard seeds	½ tspn
Urad dal	1 tblspn
Asafoetida powder	¼ tspn
Salt	to taste

METHOD OF PREPARATION

1. Clean thoroughly, wash and roughly chop spinach. Peel garlic and slice. Wash, remove stems and slit green chillies. Blend rice flour in quarter cup water.
2. Soak tamarind in half cup warm water; remove the pulp, strain and reserve. Remove stems and break red chillies into two. Wash curry leaves and pat dry.
3. Heat oil, add mustard seeds and stir-fry till they crackle. Add *urad dal*, red chillies and curry leaves. Stir well, add sliced garlic, slit green chillies and sauté for one minute. Add chopped spinach, tamarind pulp and cook on medium heat for three to four minutes, stirring frequently.
4. Sprinkle asafoetida powder and stir in dissolved rice flour. Add salt, cook for two minutes and serve hot.

MADRAS POTATO CHOPS

CRISPY SPICED POTATOES

INGREDIENTS

Potatoes	4 large sized	Curry leaves	16-20
Salt	to taste	Red chilli powder	1 tblspn
Turmeric powder	½ tspn	Coriander powder	1½ tblspns
Ginger	1 one inch piece	Rice flour	2 tblspns
Garlic	4-6 cloves	Oil	to fry + 4 tblspns

METHOD OF PREPARATION

1. Wash, peel and cut potatoes into half inch thick slices. Keep soaked in water to prevent discolouration.
2. Boil sufficient water with salt and a pinch of turmeric, add potato slices and cook on high heat for two to three minutes. Drain the parboiled potatoes immediately and spread out the slices to cool.
3. Peel, roughly chop ginger and garlic; grind with curry leaves to a smooth paste. Mix red chilli powder, turmeric powder, coriander powder, rice flour and salt with four tablespoons of oil into the ginger-garlic paste.
4. Apply this paste evenly on the parboiled potato slices and leave aside for ten minutes.
5. Heat sufficient oil in a pan and shallow-fry potato slices in small batches, without overcrowding the pan.
6. Turn over potato slices a couple of times and cook until crisp and completely cooked. Drain well on an absorbent kitchen paper and serve hot.

Chef's Tip: *Instead of shallow-frying you can also pan-roast these potato slices with very little oil.*

INGREDIENTS

Bottle gourd (*Lauki*)	1 kg
Salt	to taste
Gram flour (*Besan*)	¼ cup
Red chilli powder	1 tspn
Tamarind with seeds	10-12 pieces
Oil	for deep-frying
Gravy	
Onions	2 medium sized
Dry whole red chillies	6-8
Ginger	2 one inch pieces
Garlic	6-8 cloves
Tomatoes	2 medium sized
Fresh coriander leaves	a few sprigs
Oil	4 tblspns
Turmeric powder	½ tspn
Coriander powder	2 tblspns
Cumin powder	1 tspn
Salt	to taste
Garam masala powder	½ tspn

METHOD OF PREPARATION

1. Peel and grate the bottle gourd. Mix half teaspoon salt and keep aside for fifteen minutes. Squeeze to remove excess water. Add *besan* and red chilli powder; mix to make dough. Divide it into ten to twelve equal portions.
2. Stuff one piece of tamarind into each portion of this mixture. Moisten your palm with water and shape the stuffed portion into a ball.
3. Heat oil in a *kadai* and deep-fry the prepared *koftas* in small batches for two to three minutes or until golden brown in colour with a crisp exterior. Drain and keep on an absorbent paper.
4. Peel and finely chop onions. Clean and remove stems from red chillies. Peel ginger and garlic. Grind to a fine paste along with red chillies.
5. Wash and puree tomatoes in a blender. Clean, wash and finely chop fresh coriander leaves.
6. Heat oil in a pan, add chopped onions and sauté until they turn light golden brown. Add ginger, garlic and red chilli paste; stir-fry briefly.
7. Add turmeric powder, coriander powder, cumin powder. Continue to cook on medium heat for one minute, stirring continuously.
8. Stir in tomato puree and cook on high heat, stirring continuously till oil begins to separate. Add two cups of water and bring it to a boil. Add salt, reduce heat and simmer for five minutes.
9. Gently add the fried *koftas* and simmer for another three to four minutes.
10. Sprinkle *garam masala* powder and serve garnished with chopped fresh coriander leaves.

BEANS PARUPPU USLI

FRENCH BEANS WITH DOUBLE COOKED DALS

INGREDIENTS

French beans	250 gms
Salt	to taste
Green chillies	2
Til oil	4-5 tblspns
Mustard seeds	½ tspn
Dry whole red chillies	2
Urad dal	1 tspn
Curry leaves	8-10
Turmeric powder	½ tspn

Dal paste

Chana dal	¼ cup
Urad dal	2 tblspns
Toor dal	¼ cup
Moong dal	2 tblspns
Dry whole red chillies	6
Salt	1 tspn
Asafoetida powder	¼ tspn

METHOD OF PREPARATION

1. Wash, string and cut French beans into half centimetre sized dices. Cook beans in salted boiling water for two to three minutes. Drain well and reserve. Wash, remove stems and finely chop green chillies.
2. Soak all the *dal*s for about twenty minutes, drain and grind to a thick paste with red chillies, salt and asafoetida power, sprinkling water if required.
3. Apply a little oil on a piece of banana leaf which has been cut according to the size of the steamer or pressure-cooker. Spread *dal* paste evenly on it and steam in a cooker for fifteen minutes or until cooked. Insert a toothpick or needle into the *dal* mixture and if it comes out clean then it is cooked.
4. Turn out cooked *dal* on a large plate and cool. Crumble cooked *dal* to a coarse powder with your palm and fingers. If *dal* is dry and solid, then you can blend it in a food processor briefly.
5. Heat oil in a shallow pan, temper with mustard seeds, red chillies, *urad dal* and curry leaves.
6. Stir-fry briefly and add turmeric powder and chopped green chillies and sauté.
7. Add the cooked beans and crumbled *dal* mixture. Toss on high heat for two to three minutes. Reduce heat and cook, stirring frequently for five to six minutes or until the beans and *dal* start sizzling.
8. Adjust seasoning and serve hot.

INGREDIENTS

Carrot	1 medium sized	Green peas, shelled	¼ cup
White pumpkin	200 gms	Curry leaves	10-12
Raw banana	1 medium sized	Coconut oil	2 tblspns
Yam	100 gms	**Paste**	
French beans	6-8	Fresh coconut, scraped	½ cup
Broad beans	6-8	Green chillies	4
Drumstick	1	Cumin seeds	1½ tspns
Salt	to taste	Rice	1 tblspn
Yogurt	1½ cups		

METHOD OF PREPARATION

1. Wash and peel carrot, white pumpkin, raw banana and yam. String French beans and broad beans. Cut these vegetables into finger sized batons measuring not more than two inches in length. Wash and cut drumstick into finger sized batons.
2. Boil yam separately in salted water, drain and reserve.
3. Grind scraped coconut, green chillies, cumin seeds and rice with a little water to a fine paste. Whisk yogurt with this paste and keep aside.
4. Boil rest of the vegetables and curry leaves in one and a half cups salted water. When the vegetables are almost done, add the yogurt mixture and stir thoroughly.
5. Bring to simmering point and remove from heat. Lace with coconut oil and serve.

Chef's Tip: *If you do not like the smell of raw coconut oil, then heat up the oil, add curry leaves and temper the* aviyal. *You can also add raw mango to* aviyal, *in which case, reduce the yogurt to one cup only. Avoid reheating* aviyal.

58

INGREDIENTS

Ladies' fingers	400 gms	Pomegranate seed powder	2 tblspns
Onions	2 medium sized	*Garam masala* powder	½ tspn
Red chilli powder	1 tspn	Salt	to taste
Coriander powder	1 tblspn	Oil	½ cup
Turmeric powder	½ tspn	Lemon juice	1 tblspn

METHOD OF PREPARATION

1. Wash, wipe and trim ladies' fingers. Make a deep slit on one side of the ladies' fingers to create a pocket.
2. Peel and finely slice onions. Mix red chilli powder, coriander powder, turmeric powder, pomegranate seed powder, *garam masala* powder and salt with four tablespoons oil to make a thick paste.
3. Stuff the ladies' fingers liberally with this *masala* paste.
4. Heat oil in a pan and sauté sliced onions for two to three minutes or until they turn translucent. Gently slide in the stuffed ladies' fingers and cook on medium heat for five minutes, turning them occasionally.
5. Sprinkle lemon juice and serve hot.

Tomato Paruppu Rasam, Dahi Shorba

Sarson Ka Saag, Makki Ki Roti

INGREDIENTS

Fresh mustard leaves (*Sarson ka Saag*) .... 2 medium sized bundles
Spinach leaves (optional) .... ½ medium sized bundle
Bathua leaves (optional) .... ¼ medium sized bundle
Onions .... 2 medium sized
Garlic .... 6-8 cloves
Ginger .... 2 one inch pieces
Green chillies 4-6
Cornmeal .... 2 tblspns
Oil .... 2 tblspns
Red chilli powder .... 1 tspn
Butter .... 2 tblspns
Salt .... to taste

METHOD OF PREPARATION

1. Clean, wash, drain and roughly chop mustard, spinach and *bathua* leaves.
2. Peel and finely chop onions, garlic and ginger. Wash, remove stems and roughly chop green chillies. Blend cornmeal in half cup water.
3. Heat oil in a pan, add chopped onions and sauté for two to three minutes or until they turn translucent.
4. Add chopped ginger, garlic and green chillies and stir-fry briefly. Add red chilli powder and roughly chopped mustard, spinach and *bathua* leaves. Stir in half cup water and cook on medium heat for ten minutes, stirring occasionally.
5. Mix in the blended cornmeal and cook for five to six minutes more, stirring continuously.
6. Cool the mixture lightly and grind to a coarse paste. Reheat, add butter and salt to taste.
7. Stir well and serve hot with *makki ki roti*.

Chef's Tip: *Traditionally Sarson Saag is pounded to a paste with a wooden* mathni *or* ravai, *while it is being cooked. The process is quite cumbersome and time consuming but the result is delicious.*

AMBAT BATATA

TANGY POTATO CURRY

INGREDIENTS

Potatoes	5-6 medium sized	Cumin seeds	1 tspn
Onions	3 medium sized	Turmeric powder	½ tspn
Curry leaves	6-7	Yogurt, beaten	½ cup
Fresh coriander leaves	¼ cup	*Kokam*	4-5
Green chillies	3	Fresh coconut, scraped	¼ cup
Oil	3 tblspns	Salt	to taste
Mustard seeds	½ tspn	Lemon juice	2 tspns

METHOD OF PREPARATION

1. Boil and peel potatoes. Halve each potato and further cut each half into four equal sized pieces. Peel and finely chop onions. Wash and pat dry curry leaves.
2. Clean, wash and finely chop coriander leaves. Wash, remove stems and finely chop green chillies.
3. Heat oil in a pan; add mustard seeds and let them crackle. Add cumin seeds and stir-fry briefly. Add curry leaves and green chillies, stir. Add chopped onions immediately and sauté till golden brown in colour.
4. Add turmeric powder, potato cubes and stir-fry for one or two minutes. Stir in yogurt, *kokam* pieces, half of the chopped fresh coriander leaves and scraped coconut, salt and lemon juice. Reduce heat and simmer for one or two minutes.
5. Garnish with reserved scraped coconut and fresh coriander leaves and serve hot.

Chef's Tip : *You may replace* kokam *with tamarind.*

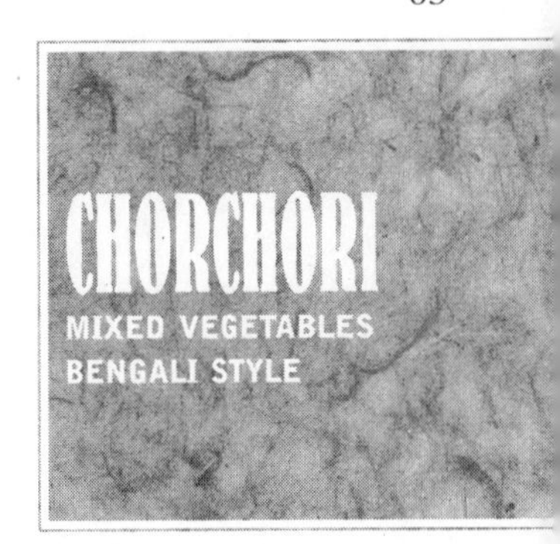

INGREDIENTS

Ingredient	Quantity
Cauliflower	¼
Potatoes	2 medium sized
Sweet potato	1 medium sized
Red pumpkin	100 gms
Brinjal	1 medium sized
French beans	6-8
Spinach leaves	6-8
Green chillies	2
Mustard oil	1 ½ tblspns
Panch phoron	1 ½ tspns
Red chilli powder	½ tspn
Turmeric powder	¼ tspn
Sugar	½ tspn
Salt	to taste

METHOD OF PREPARATION

1. Wash and separate the cauliflower into small florets. Peel and cut the potatoes, sweet potato, and red pumpkin into half inch sized pieces. Wash and cut the brinjal into half inch sized pieces.
2. String and cut the French beans into half inch sized pieces. Clean, wash fresh spinach leaves two to three times in running water and shred. Wash, remove stems and slit green chillies
3. Heat one tablespoon mustard oil in a pan till it reaches smoking point. Remove, cool and heat the oil again on medium heat.
4. Add *panch phoron* and when it starts crackling add red chilli powder, stir briefly and add the prepared vegetables. Stir and add turmeric powder, slit green chillies, sugar and salt to taste. Reduce heat, cover and cook for eight to ten minutes, stirring occasionally or till potato pieces are cooked.
5. Add half tablespoon of raw mustard oil and stir-fry for one minute or till *chorchori* is dry.

Chef's Tip: *Panch phoron is a mixture of equal quantities of mustard seeds, cumin seeds, fenugreek, fennel seeds and* shahi jeera.

64

KACHA KOLAR DALNA

RAW BANANA KOFTA CURRY

INGREDIENTS

Raw bananas ....4 medium sized
Ginger ....2 one inch pieces
Garlic ....6-8 cloves
Fresh coriander leaves .... ¼ cup
Onion ....1 large sized
Tomato ....1 medium sized
Gram flour *(Besan)* ....2 tblspns
Red chilli powder ....1 tspn
Salt ....to taste
Oil ....1 tblspn + for frying
Bay leaf 1
Turmeric powder .... ½ tspn
Garam masala powder .... ½ tspn

METHOD OF PREPARATION

1. Wash, boil and cool raw bananas. Peel and mash thoroughly.
2. Peel ginger and garlic and grind to a fine paste. Clean, wash and finely chop fresh coriander leaves. Peel and grate the onion. Wash and finely chop the tomato.
3. Mix mashed bananas, chopped coriander leaves, gram flour, one teaspoon ginger-garlic paste, half teaspoon red chilli powder and salt to taste. Knead the dough and divide into ten to twelve equal sized portions. Shape them into round *koftas*.
4. Heat oil in a *kadai* and deep-fry *koftas* on medium heat till golden brown. Drain on an absorbent kitchen towel.
5. Heat oil in a pan; add bay leaf and grated onion. Sauté till onion turns translucent and add remaining ginger-garlic paste and stir-fry briefly.
6. Add the remaining red chilli powder, turmeric powder, chopped tomatoes and cook on low heat, stirring continuously till oil separates.
7. Add two cups of water and salt to taste and bring the gravy to a boil. Reduce heat and add fried *koftas*. Simmer for five minutes. Stir in the *garam masala* powder and serve hot.

INGREDIENTS

Small brinjals	8-10
Onions	2 medium sized
Tamarind	1 lemon sized ball
Fresh coriander leaves	¼ cup
Fresh coconut, scraped	¾ cup
Oil	4 tblspns
Dry coconut, grated	¼ cup
Sesame seeds	2 tblspns
Roasted peanuts, skinned	¼ cup
Cumin seeds	½ tspn
Coriander seeds	1 tspn
Goda masala	2 tspns
Salt	to taste
Turmeric powder	¼ tspn
Red chilli powder	1 ½ tspns
Mustard seeds	½ tspn
Curry leaves	6-8

METHOD OF PREPARATION

1. Wash and slit brinjals into four, keeping the stems intact. Keep in water.
2. Peel and thinly slice onions. Soak tamarind in half a cup of warm water for half an hour, remove the pulp, strain and keep aside.
3. Clean, wash and finely chop fresh coriander leaves. Reserve one tablespoon each of the scraped coconut and chopped coriander leaves for garnish.
4. Heat one teaspoon oil in a pan and add sliced onions. Stir-fry onions briefly.
5. Add grated dry coconut, sesame seeds, peanuts, cumin seeds and coriander seeds and cook on medium heat for two minutes, stirring continuously or till dry coconut changes to light golden in colour.
6. Cool and grind to a coarse paste adding a little water. Combine this paste with *goda masala*, salt, turmeric powder, red chilli powder, fresh scraped coconut, chopped fresh coriander leaves and tamarind pulp. Stuff this prepared mixture into brinjals.
7. Heat remaining oil in a pan, add mustard seeds and let them crackle. Add curry leaves and gently place stuffed brinjals.
8. Cook for two to three minutes. Gently turn brinjals once or twice to ensure even cooking. Add one cup of water, bring it to a boil.
9. Reduce heat and cook covered for eight to ten minutes or till brinjals are cooked and soft. Most of the stuffing will leave the brinjals and form the gravy for the dish.
10. Serve hot, garnished with fresh coriander leaves.

INGREDIENTS

White radish with leaves	4-5 medium sized
Green chillies	4
Fresh coriander leaves	a few sprigs
Gram flour (*Besan*)	¼ cup
Oil	2 tblspns
Mustard seeds	½ tspn
Asafoetida powder	¼ tspn
Urad dal	1 ½ tspns
Turmeric powder	¼ tspn
Salt	to taste
Sugar	½ tspn

METHOD OF PREPARATION

1. Wash, peel and grate white radish. Clean, wash and finely chop the radish leaves.
2. Wash remove stems and finely chop the green chillies. Clean, wash and finely chop fresh coriander leaves.
3. Dry roast gram flour in a pan on low flame, stirring continuously for three to four minutes. Ensure that there is no raw flavour.
4. Heat oil in a pan, add mustard seeds and let them crackle. Add asafoetida powder and *urad dal,* stir-fry briefly.
5. Add chopped green chillies, turmeric powder, white radish with leaves, salt and sugar. Mix well and cook covered for six to seven minutes on medium heat, stirring occasionally.
6. When radish is cooked and the mixture dries up, sprinkle gram flour and continue to cook on medium heat for a couple of minutes, stirring occasionally.
7. Serve hot, garnished with chopped fresh coriander leaves.

INGREDIENTS

Matki (*Mauth*)	1 cup
Onions	2 medium sized
Fresh coriander leaves	a few sprigs
Fresh coconut, scraped	2 tblspns
Oil	3 tblspns
Mustard seeds	½ tspn
Curry leaves	6-8
Turmeric powder	½ tspn
Red chilli powder	½ tspn
Goda masala	1 tspn
Jaggery, grated	1 tspn
Salt	to taste
For paste	
Garlic	6-7 cloves
Green chillies	3-4
Cumin seeds	1 tspn
Fresh coconut, scraped	¼ cup

METHOD OF PREPARATION

1. Clean, wash and soak *matki* overnight in four cups of water.
2. Peel garlic. Wash, remove stems and finely chop green chillies. Peel onions and chop finely. Clean, wash and finely chop fresh coriander leaves.
3. Dry roast cumin seeds on a *tawa*. Grind roasted cumin seeds, green chillies, coconut and garlic to a fine paste.
4. Heat oil in a pan, add mustard seeds and allow them to crackle. Add curry leaves and chopped onions. Sauté onions, stirring continuously till they turn light golden.
5. Add the paste and cook on medium heat for three to four minutes.
6. Add turmeric powder, red chilli powder, *goda masala*, jaggery and salt. Stir well.
7. Add drained *matki*, mix well and add just enough water to cover the *matki* mixture.
8. Bring it to a boil and continue cooking on medium heat, stirring occasionally till *matki* is cooked.
9. Serve hot garnished with chopped fresh coriander leaves and scraped coconut.

68

PINDI CHHOLAY

SPICED CHICKPEAS FROM ERSTWHILE PUNJAB

INGREDIENTS

Chickpeas (*Kabuli Chana*) ... 1½ cups
Tea leaves ... 1 tblspn
Tomatoes ... 2 medium sized
Green chillies ... 4-6
Ginger ... 2 one inch pieces
Garlic ... 8-10 cloves
Coriander powder ... 2 tblspns
Cumin powder ... 2 tblspns
Red chilli powder ... 1½ tspns
Turmeric powder ... ½ tspn
Amchur powder ... ½ tspn
Cumin seeds ... 2 tblspns
Pomegranate seeds (*Anardana*) ... 1 tblspn
Oil ... ½ cup
Salt ... to taste
Garam masala powder ... 1 tspn

METHOD OF PREPARATION

1. Wash and soak chickpeas in sufficient water overnight. Tie tea leaves in muslin cloth to form a bundle. Wash and cut tomatoes into four to six pieces. Wash, remove stems and slit green chillies. Peel ginger, garlic and grind to a fine paste.
2. Drain the water from the chickpeas; add six to eight cups water, salt and tea leaves tied in muslin. Pressure cook for twenty minutes or until soft and completely cooked. Drain the cooked chickpeas and reserve the cooking liquor.
3. Mix together coriander powder, cumin powder, red chilli powder, turmeric powder, and *amchur*. Dry roast cumin seeds till they turn dark brown. Dry roast *anardana* and grind to a powder alongwith roasted cumin seeds.
4. Heat four tablespoons oil in a *kadai*, add slit green chillies, and ginger-garlic paste. Stir-fry briefly. Add the mixed spice powder and stir-fry for half a minute. Stir in half cup of the reserved cooking liquor and cook for two minutes.
5. Add the cooked chickpeas, salt to taste, one cup reserved cooking liquor and cook on high heat for three to four minutes, stirring occasionally. Top it with tomatoes, sprinkle *garam masala* powder, roasted cumin and *anardana* powder.
6. Heat the remaining oil to smoking point and pour over the prepared chickpeas.
7. Stir well, adjust seasoning and serve hot.

Dum Paneer Kalimirch, Pindi Chholay

Lebsuni Tikki

INGREDIENTS

Green chillies	2	Coriander powder	2 tspns
Ginger	1 one inch piece	Cumin powder	1 tspn
Oil	2 tblspns	Red chilli powder	½ tspn
Asafoetida powder	¼ tspn	Salt	to taste
Mustard seeds	½ tspn	*Garam masala* powder	½ tspn
Green peas, shelled	1 ½ cups		

METHOD OF PREPARATION

1. Wash, remove stems and roughly chop green chillies. Peel ginger and grind to a fine paste along with green chillies.
2. Heat oil in a pan and add asafoetida powder. Add mustard seeds immediately and stir-fry till they start crackling. Add ginger, green chilli paste and shelled green peas. Sauté for two minutes, stirring continuously.
3. Add coriander powder, cumin powder and red chilli powder. Cook on medium heat for one minute, stirring continuously.
4. Stir in two cups of water and bring it to a boil. Reduce heat and simmer for ten to fifteen minutes, stirring occasionally or till green peas are completely cooked.
5. Stir in salt and *garam masala* powder and serve hot.

RISHIPANCHAMI BHAJEE

ASSORTED VEGETABLES, ESPECIALLY COOKED ON RISHIPANCHAMI DAY

INGREDIENTS

Ridge gourd (*Ghosala* or *Turia*) .... 1 medium sized
Cucumber .... 2 medium sized
Red pumpkin .... 150 gms
Snake gourd .... ½ small sized
Ladies' fingers 10-12
Fresh corn kernels .... ½ cup
Green chillies 5-6
Fresh coriander leaves .... ½ cup
Oil .... 3 tblspns
Salt .... to taste
Fresh coconut, scraped .... ¾ cup

For tempering

Pure *ghee* .... 1 tblspn
Cumin seeds .... 1 tspn

METHOD OF PREPARATION

1. Peel, remove seeds and cut *turia*, cucumber, red pumpkin and snake gourd into one inch sized cubes.
2. Wipe ladies' fingers with a moist cloth, trim both ends and cut each into four to five pieces. Boil corn kernels till almost cooked. Drain and keep aside.
3. Wash, remove stems and slit green chillies. Clean, wash and finely chop fresh coriander leaves.
4. Heat a pan and add all the prepared vegetables including the cooked corn kernels, slit green chillies, chopped coriander and scraped coconut. Add sufficient water to cover the vegetables and bring it to a boil.
5. Reduce heat, cover and simmer for eight to ten minutes or till vegetables are well cooked.
6. Heat pure *ghee* in a tempering pan, add cumin seeds and when they start to change colour, pour the tempering over the vegetables.

INGREDIENTS

Carrots	2 medium sized	Curry leaves	10-12
Potatoes	2 medium sized	Fresh coconut, scraped	2 cups
French beans	6-8	Green peas, shelled	½ cup
Cauliflower	1 small sized	Oil	4 tblspns
Salt	to taste	Coconut oil	2 tblspns
Onions	2 medium sized	Bay leaves	2
Green chillies	4	Star anise	2
Ginger	1 one inch piece	Cinnamon	2 one inch sticks
Garlic	4-6 cloves	*Garam masala* powder	½ tspn

METHOD OF PREPARATION

1. Wash, peel and cut carrots and potatoes into one inch sized pieces. Wash, string and cut beans into one inch sized pieces. Clean and cut cauliflower into small florets and soak in warm salted water for fifteen minutes and drain.
2. Peel and finely chop the onions. Wash, remove stems and slit the green chillies.
3. Peel ginger and garlic and grind to a fine paste. Wash and pat dry curry leaves.
4. Soak the scraped coconut in two cups of warm water, grind and squeeze to remove milk. Repeat this process two more times but with only one cup water to get a second and third extract.
5. Heat sufficient water and boil carrots, potatoes, French beans, cauliflower and green peas, individually until almost cooked.
6. Heat oil in a pan, add coconut oil, bay leaves, star anise and cinnamon and stir-fry briefly. Add chopped onions, curry leaves and slit green chillies and sauté for three to four minutes or until the onions start turning light brown.
7. Add cooked carrots, potatoes, French beans, cauliflower and green peas and stir-fry for two minutes. Stir in the third extract of coconut milk and bring to a boil.
8. Reduce heat and simmer for two to three minutes. Add the second extract of coconut milk and cook on medium heat till the liquid is reduced to half the quantity.
9. Add salt, remove from heat and stir in the first extract of coconut milk.
10. Reheat on medium heat for two minutes, sprinkle *garam masala* powder and serve hot.

Chef's Tip: *You can make this with only root vegetables like potatoes, carrots, etc. This preparation is traditionally accompanied by* aappams.

PHOOL GOBHI SAMBHARI

CAULIFLOWER IN COCONUT MILK

INGREDIENTS

Cauliflower	1 medium sized (approx. 800 gms)	Asafoetida powder	¼ tspn
Onions	3 medium sized	Turmeric powder	½ tspn
Fresh coriander leaves	a few sprigs	Red chilli powder	1 tspn
Tamarind	1 lemon sized ball	Salt	to taste
Fresh coconut, scraped	¾ cup	Sugar	½ tspn
Oil	4 tblspns	*Pathare prabhu masala*	1 ½ tspns
Cumin seeds	½ tspn	Cashewnuts	12-15
		Gram flour (*Besan*)	¼ cup

METHOD OF PREPARATION

1. Wash and cut cauliflower into small florets. Peel and finely chop the onions. Clean, wash and chop coriander leaves.
2. Soak tamarind in one cup warm water for half an hour, remove the pulp, strain and keep aside.
3. Reserve one tablespoon of the scraped coconut for garnish. Soak the remaining scraped coconut in one and half cups warm water, grind and extract milk.
4. Heat oil in a pan, add cumin seeds and when they start to change colour, add asafoetida powder and chopped onions. Sauté until onions turn soft and translucent.
5. Add turmeric powder, red chilli powder, salt, sugar, *pathare prabhu masala*, cashewnuts and cauliflower florets. Mix well.
6. Add one cup water and bring it to a boil. Reduce heat, cover and simmer for six to eight minutes.
7. Dissolve gram flour in half the quantity of coconut milk. Mix it well to ensure that there are no lumps and add this to the cauliflower mixture.
8. Increase the heat and bring it to a boil. Continue to cook on medium heat till cauliflower is cooked, stirring occasionally. Stir in the remaining coconut milk.
9. Serve hot, garnished with fresh coriander leaves and scraped coconut.

INGREDIENTS

Whole coriander seeds	8 tblspns
Cumin seeds	1½ tblspns
Mustard seeds	1½ tblspns
Whole wheat	2 tblspns
Chana dal	2 tblspns
Dry whole red chillies	16-20
Turmeric powder	1 tspn
Fenugreek seeds	½ tspn
Asafoetida powder	a pinch
Peppercorns	1 tspn

METHOD OF PREPARATION

1. Dry roast all ingredients except asafoetida powder, one at a time.
2. Cool and grind to a fine powder. Store in an airtight container.

76

KACHCHI MAKAI DHINGRI

TENDER BABYCORN AND MUSHROOM

INGREDIENTS

Fresh button mushrooms .... 10-12 medium sized
Fresh baby corn ..... 10-12 small sized
Capsicum .... 1 medium sized
Onion .... 1 medium sized
Ginger .... 1 one inch piece
Garlic .... 6-8 cloves
Green chillies 2
Tomato .... 1 medium sized
Fresh coriander leaves .... ¼ cup
Oil .... 4 tblspns
Bay leaves 2
Red chilli powder .... 1 tblspn
Coriander powder .... 2 tblspns
Tumeric powder .... 1 tspn
Cumin powder .... ½ tblspn
Sweet corn niblets .... ½ cup
Salt .... to taste
Garam masala powder .... 1 tspn

METHOD OF PREPARATION

1 Clean, wash and cut mushroom into quarters. Clean, wash and cut baby corn into half inch sized pieces. Wash, halve, remove seeds and cut capsicum into half-inch broad strips.

2 Peel and grate onion. Peel ginger and garlic; grind to a fine paste. Wash, remove stems and slit green chillies. Wash and finely chop tomato. Clean, wash and finely chop fresh coriander leaves.

3 Heat oil in a pan, add bay leaves, grated onion, slit green chillies and sauté for three to four minutes or until the onion turns light brown in colour. Add ginger-garlic paste and stir-fry briefly.

4 Add red chilli, coriander, turmeric and cumin powders. Mix well and add chopped tomato. Cook on high heat for two to three minutes, stirring continuously. Add mushroom, baby corn, sweet corn niblets and salt to taste and continue to cook for five minutes on medium heat.

5 Add capsicum strips, toss well and cook for two minutes on medium heat, stirring continuously. Sprinkle chopped coriander leaves, *garam masala* powder and serve hot.

INGREDIENTS

Fresh button mushrooms	20-24	Melon seeds	1 tblspn
Onions	2 medium sized	Yogurt	2 tblspns
Ginger	2 one inch pieces	Oil	4 tblspns
Garlic	4-6 cloves	Red chilli powder	1 tspn
Fresh coriander leaves	¼ cup	Coriander powder	1 tspn
Tomatoes	2 medium sized	Cumin powder	½ tspn
Cashewnuts	10-12	Salt	to taste
Poppy seeds	1 tblspn	*Garam masala* powder	½ tspn

METHOD OF PREPARATION

1. Clean, wash, drain and cut button mushrooms into four. Peel and finely chop onions. Peel ginger and garlic; grind to a fine paste. Clean, wash and finely chop fresh coriander leaves.
2. Wash, roughly chop and puree tomatoes in a blender. Soak cashewnuts, poppy seeds and melon seeds in hot water for ten minutes, drain and grind to a fine paste. Whisk yogurt and keep aside.
3. Heat oil in a pan, add chopped onions and sauté for two to three minutes or until light brown in colour. Add ginger-garlic paste and stir-fry briefly.
4. Add red chilli powder, coriander powder, cumin powder and salt. Stir well and add tomato puree. Cook on medium heat stirring continuously for two minutes or until the oil separates. Add mushrooms and sauté for two minutes on high heat.
5. Dilute cashewnut, poppy seed and melon seed paste in yogurt and one and a half cups water and add to the mushroom mixture. Bring to a boil, reduce heat and simmer for five minutes or until the mushrooms are cooked.
6. Sprinkle *garam masala* powder and chopped coriander leaves and serve hot.

PANEER TAMATAR KA KHUT

COTTAGE CHEESE IN TOMATO CURRY

INGREDIENTS

Tomatoes	8-10 medium sized
Ginger	2 one inch pieces
Garlic	10-12 cloves
Paneer	250 gms
Curry leaves	20
Chana dal, roasted	¼ cup
Tamarind	½ lemon sized ball
Dry whole red chillies	6-8
Til oil	1 tblspn
Mustard seeds	1 tspn
Cumin seeds	1 tspn
Cinnamon	3 one inch sticks
Turmeric powder	1 tspn
Coriander powder	2 tspns
Cumin powder	1 tspn
Salt	to taste
Coconut milk	¼ cup

METHOD OF PREPARATION

1. Wash and roughly chop tomatoes. Scrape, wash and roughly chop ginger. Peel and crush garlic. Cut *paneer* into finger sized batons. Clean, wash and pat dry curry leaves.
2. Grind roasted *chana dal* into fine powder. Soak tamarind in half a cup of warm water for half an hour, remove the pulp, strain and keep aside.
3. Heat a pan and add chopped tomatoes alongwith chopped ginger, crushed garlic and red chillies. Add half a cup of water and bring it to a boil.
4. Reduce heat, cover and simmer for fifteen to twenty minutes or till it is reduced to half the quantity. Remove the tomato mixture from the heat, cool and pass through a fine mesh or a soup strainer.
5. Heat oil in a pan, add mustard and cumin seeds, stir-fry briefly until mustard seeds begin to crackle. Add curry leaves, cinnamon, turmeric powder, coriander powder and cumin powder. Stir-fry briefly.
6. Immediately add strained tomato mixture. Bring it to a boil and stir in tamarind pulp and salt. Add roasted *chana dal* powder and mix thoroughly.
7. Reduce heat and stir in coconut milk and add *paneer* pieces. Simmer for two to three minutes and serve hot.

Shakkarkand Chaat / Phalon Ka Kachumber

Kashmiri Dahi Baingan, Aloo Posto

INGREDIENTS

Brinjals, long variety	6-8 medium sized
Yogurt	2 cups
Salt	to taste
Oil	2 tblspns + to deep-fry brinjals
Asafoetida powder	¼ tspn
Green cardamoms	3-4
Fennel powder	1 tblspn
Ginger powder	½ tblspn
Kashmiri red chilli powder	2 tspns

METHOD OF PREPARATION

1. Wash and cut brinjals into quarters lengthwise and keep in water till further use. Whisk yogurt and salt together.
2. Heat sufficient oil in a *kadai*. Drain, pat dry and deep-fry brinjals till light brown. Transfer to an absorbent kitchen towel.
3. Heat two tablespoons of oil in a pan, add asafoetida powder and green cardamoms. Stir-fry briefly and immediately add the whisked yogurt. Stir in fennel, ginger and red chilli powder.
4. Cook on medium heat for two to three minutes and add fried brinjals. Reduce heat and cook covered for three to four minutes. Adjust seasoning and serve hot.

INGREDIENTS

Potatoes	5-6 medium sized	Salt	to taste
Poppy seeds	4 tblspns	Sugar	½ tspn
Mustard oil	2 tblspns	Green chillies	2
Nigella seeds *(Kalonji)*	½ tspn	Pure *ghee* (optional)	1 tspn

METHOD OF PREPARATION

1. Peel and cut the potatoes into one inch sized pieces. Keep them in water. Soak poppy seeds in one cup warm water for fifteen to twenty minutes. Drain and grind to a fine paste.
2. Heat mustard oil in a pan till it reaches smoking point. Remove, cool and heat the oil again on medium heat. Add *kalonji* and stir-fry briefly. Add potato pieces and cook on medium heat for five minutes, stirring frequently.
3. Add the poppy seeds paste, stir and add half cup water, cover and cook on low heat till the potatoes are almost done. Remove the lid, add salt, sugar and slit green chillies.
4. Continue to cook for a minute more or till potatoes are completely cooked, stir in pure *ghee* (optional) and serve hot.

INGREDIENTS

Malai paneer	400 gms	Bay leaves	2
Green chillies	2-3	Cinnamon	1 one inch stick
Ginger	1 one inch piece	Green cardamoms	3-4
Garlic	4-5 cloves	Cloves	3-4
Fresh coriander leaves	½ cup	Coriander powder	2 tblspns
Fresh mint leaves	¼ cup	Cumin powder	1 tspn
Yogurt	1 cup	Salt	to taste
Onions	2 medium sized	Fresh cream	½ cup
Oil	to deep-fry onions	Peppercorns, crushed	1 tblspn
Pure *ghee*	2 tblspns	*Garam masala* powder	1 tspn

METHOD OF PREPARATION

1. Cut *paneer* into one inch sized cubes. Wash and remove stems of green chillies. Peel ginger and garlic and grind to a fine paste along with the green chillies. Wash and finely chop the fresh coriander and mint leaves. Whisk yogurt to a smooth consistency.
2. Peel and finely slice the onions. Heat oil in a *kadai* and deep-fry the sliced onions in hot oil, till golden brown, drain on an absorbent kitchen towel and cool.
3. Grind the fried onions with two tablespoons water to a smooth paste.
4. Heat pure *ghee* in a narrow-mouthed *handi*, add bay leaves, cinnamon, cardamoms and cloves and stir-fry briefly. Add ginger, garlic, chilli paste and sauté on high heat for half a minute.
5. Add the brown onion paste, whisked yogurt, coriander powder, cumin powder and salt to taste. Stir well, add one cup water and cook on high flame, stirring briefly till the gravy starts boiling.
6. Add the *paneer* pieces and mix in the chopped coriander and mint leaves. Stir in the fresh cream and crushed black peppercorns. Sprinkle *garam masala* powder.
7. Cover the *handi* with a tight-fitting lid and seal using whole meal flour (*atta* dough) or alternately, seal tightly with aluminium foil.
8. Preheat oven to 200 degrees Celsius. Place sealed *handi* in the preheated oven and cook for ten to fifteen minutes.
9. Open the *handi* just before serving and serve immediately.

***Chef's Tip:** Just before sealing, transfer the* paneer *to four single portion copper handis and proceed as above. Let the guests open their* handis *at the dining-table to enjoy the delicate fragrance of* dum *cooking.*

SAMBHAR

FAMOUS SOUTH INDIAN DAL WITH VEGETABLES

INGREDIENTS

Toor dal	½ cup
Turmeric powder	¼ tspn
Til oil	4 tblspns
Tamarind	1 lemon sized ball
Green chillies	4
Drumsticks	2
Fresh coriander leaves	¼ cup
Curry leaves	10-12
Mustard seeds	½ tspn
Dry whole red chillies	4
Fenugreek seeds (optional)	½ tspn
Asafoetida powder	¼ tspn
Sambhar powder	1½ tspns
Salt	to taste
Rice flour	1 tspn

METHOD OF PREPARATION

1. Wash and pressure-cook the *dal* in two and a half cups of water with turmeric powder and one teaspoon oil. Mash the cooked *dal* lightly with a wooden spoon.
2. Soak tamarind in one cup warm water, remove the pulp, strain and keep aside.
3. Wash, remove stems and slit the green chillies. Wash and cut drumsticks into two and half inch pieces. Wash and chop the coriander leaves. Wash and pat dry curry leaves.
4. Heat oil in a thick-bottomed pan; add mustard seeds, stir-fry till they start to crackle. Add red chillies, fenugreek seeds and asafoetida powder.
5. Add slit green chillies, curry leaves and drumsticks, and cook on medium heat, stirring briefly.
6. Stir in the tamarind pulp, add *sambhar* powder, salt and one cup water.
7. Reduce heat and simmer for six to eight minutes or till drumsticks are cooked. Add boiled *dal* and simmer for two to three minutes.
8. Blend rice flour in quarter cup water and add to the *sambhar.* Stir well and cook further for two to three minutes, stirring occasionally.
9. Sprinkle chopped coriander leaves and serve hot.

Chef's Tip: *You can use different vegetables like white radish, ladies' finger, pumpkin, brinjal,* sambhar *onion, etc., either individually or in any combination. In south of India, each family has its own style of making* sambhar.

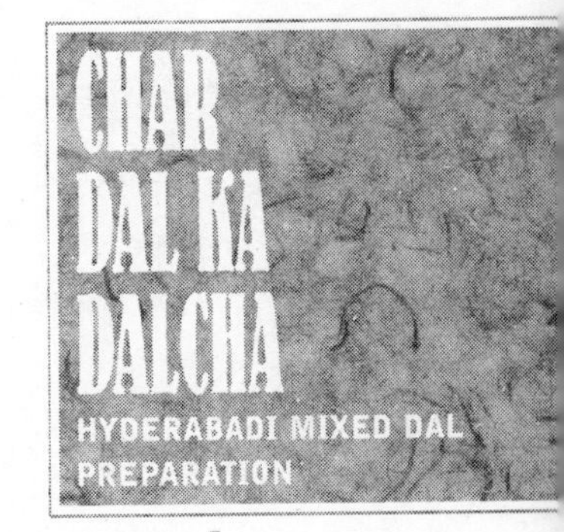

INGREDIENTS

Chana dal	¼ cup
Masoor dal	2 tblspns
Toor dal	¼ cup
Moong dal	2 tblspns
Turmeric powder	1 tspn
Red chilli powder	1 ½ tspns
Salt	to taste
Onions	2 medium sized
Green chillies	5-6
Ginger	1 one inch piece
Garlic	6-8 cloves
Curry leaves	12-15
White pumpkin	400 gms
Tamarind	1 lemon sized ball
Oil	3 tblspns
Pure *ghee*	2 tblspns
Cumin seeds	1 tspn
Dry whole red chillies	5-6

METHOD OF PREPARATION

1. Wash and soak all the *dals* in plenty of water for at least half an hour. Drain and add half teaspoon turmeric powder, half teaspoon chilli powder, salt and four cups of water. Pressure cook for four to five minutes or till it is completely cooked.
2. Peel and finely slice onions. Wash, remove stems and slit green chillies. Peel ginger and grind to a fine paste. Peel and finely chop garlic. Clean, wash and pat dry curry leaves.
3. Peel, scoop out seeds and cut white pumpkin into one inch sized pieces. Soak tamarind in one cup warm water for half an hour, remove the pulp, strain and keep aside.
4. Heat oil in a pan, add sliced onions. Sauté till they turn light brown. Add ginger paste, the remaining chilli powder and turmeric powder and slit green chillies. Stir-fry briefly and add white pumpkin pieces.
5. Sauté for three to four minutes and add the cooked *dals*. Cook covered on medium heat for about ten minutes or till the white pumpkin pieces are tender. Add tamarind pulp and half a cup of water and cook on medium heat for four to five minutes, stirring occasionally. Reduce heat and simmer for another five minutes.
6. Heat *ghee* in a tempering pan, add cumin seeds and when they start changing colour add red chillies broken into two and curry leaves. Stir-fry briefly and add chopped garlic till it turns light brown.
7. Temper the *dal* with this mixture and cover it with a lid immediately to trap the aroma.
8. Adjust seasoning and serve hot.

THENGAI SADHAM

COCONUT RICE

INGREDIENTS

Rice	1½ cups
Onion	1 medium sized
Ginger	1 one inch piece
Green Chillies	2
Fresh coriander leaves	¼ cup
Curry leaves	10-12
Dry whole red chillies	2
Pure *ghee*	1 tblspn
Cashewnuts	6-8
Oil	4 tblspns
Mustard seeds	½ tspn
Urad dal	1 tspn
Fresh coconut, scraped	1 cup
Salt	to taste
Coconut oil (optional)	1 tspn

METHOD OF PREPARATION

1. Clean, wash and soak rice for half an hour. Boil sufficient water and cook rice, stirring frequently till almost done. Drain out excess water, spread out cooked rice on a flat plate to cool.
2. Peel and finely chop onion. Wash, peel and finely chop ginger. Wash, remove stems and finely chop green chillies. Clean, wash and finely chop fresh coriander leaves. Wash and pat dry curry leaves. Remove stems and break red chillies into two and keep.
3. Heat pure *ghee* in a tempering pan and stir-fry cashewnuts till light brown and keep aside.
4. Heat oil in a *kadai*, add mustard seeds and stir-fry till they crackle. Add *urad dal*, red chillies, curry leaves and stir-fry briefly.
5. Add chopped onion, green chillies, ginger and sauté for two to three minutes or until onion is translucent. Add scraped coconut and cook on medium heat for two minutes. Add cooked rice, salt, chopped coriander leaves and toss well to mix and heat it through.
6. Sprinkle coconut oil and serve hot garnished with fried cashewnuts.

INGREDIENTS

Rice	1½ cups
Toor dal	¾ cup
Onion	1 medium sized
Sambhar onions	8-10 small sized
Tomatoes	3 medium sized
Green chillies	3-4
Curry leaves	10-12
Tamarind	1½ lemon sized balls
Groundnut oil	5 tblspns
Turmeric powder	½ tspn
Asafoetida powder	¼ tspn
Red chilli powder	½ tspn
Salt	to taste
Mustard seeds	½ tspn
Dry whole red chillies	2
Pure *ghee*	4 tblspns
Cashewnuts	10-12
Huliyana masala	
Chana dal	¼ cup
Urad dal	2 tblspns
Green cardamoms	4
Cloves	4
Cinnamon	1 one inch stick
Fenugreek seeds	1 tspn
Cumin seeds	1 tspn
Dry whole red chillies	4

METHOD OF PREPARATION

1. Clean, wash and soak rice and *toor dal* separately for twenty minutes and drain.
2. Peel and finely slice the onions. Peel *sambhar* onions. Wash and cut tomatoes into quarters. Wash, remove stems and slit green chillies. Wash and pat dry curry leaves.
3. Soak tamarind in one cup warm water for half an hour, remove the pulp, strain and keep aside.
4. Dry roast *huliyana masala* ingredients individually on a *tawa*, mix and grind to a coarse powder.
5. Heat three tablespoons oil in a pressure cooker and sauté the onion till it turns translucent. Add slit green chillies, *sambhar* onions and stir-fry briefly. Add curry leaves and turmeric powder.
6. Add soaked rice and *dal* along with five cups of water. Bring to a boil, stirring occasionally.
7. Add tomatoes, asafoetida powder, red chilli powder, tamarind water and salt. Stir well and add the powdered *huliyana masala*. Cover and pressure-cook for five minutes.
8. Open the lid carefully and stir well. Check consistency. If it is too dry, moisten with a little warm water. Heat remaining oil and temper it with mustard seeds and red chillies.
9. Heat pure *ghee* and fry the cashewnuts to light brown and add to the rice, along with the *ghee*. Mix well and serve hot.

Chef's Tip: *You can add vegetables of your choice to Bisi bele huliyana. The consistency of this dish should be loose and porridge-like. Make this only with regular rice and not with long grain varieties like basmati, etc.*

INGREDIENTS

Rice	1 cup	Fresh coconut, scraped	¾ cup
Parboiled rice	1 cup	Baking powder	¼ tspn
Coconut water	¼ cup	Oil	to grease *aappam tawa*
Salt	to taste		

METHOD OF PREPARATION

1. Clean, wash and soak both the rice together for two to three hours. Drain and grind soaked rice to a smooth paste adding coconut water, as required.
2. Add salt, stir well and keep ground rice for at least thirty-six hours in a warm place to ferment.
3. Soak the scraped coconut in one and a half cups warm water, grind and extract thick milk. Add the coconut milk to the fermented batter and dilute it to a thick creamy consistency. Mix in the baking powder and adjust salt.
4. Heat an *aappam tawa* (small cast-iron *kadai*), brush with a little oil. Add one ladle of batter, tilt the *kadai* all around to spread the batter. The edges should be thin and the excess batter should collect at the centre.
5. Cover with a thick heavy lid and cook on medium heat for two to three minutes. Check to see if the sides start leaving the *tawa*. The edges of the *aappam* should be crisp and thin and the centre soft and spongy.
6. Serve hot with your choice of *ishtew*.

Chef's Tip: *Traditionally fresh toddy is used to ferment this batter. In the above recipe, the coconut water acts as the fermenting agent. A special type of* tawa *made in cast iron is available to make these* aappams. *You may also use a small non-stick* kadai *for this purpose.*

Kaikari Ishtew, Aappam

Narangi Shorba

INGREDIENTS

Ingredient	Quantity
Rice	1 ½ cups
Brinjals	3-4 small sized
Salt	to taste
Tendli	8-10
Fresh coriander leaves	¼ cup
Dry whole red chillies	6-7
Coriander seeds	2 tspns
Dry coconut, scraped (*Khopra*)	½ cup
Cumin seeds	1 tspn
Oil	4 tblspns
Cloves	5-6
Green cardamoms	2 -3
Bay leaves	2
Turmeric powder	1 tspn
Fried or roasted cashewnuts	8-10
Fresh coconut, scraped	2 tblspns

METHOD OF PREPARATION

1. Pick, clean and wash rice with plenty of water two to three times. Soak in water for thirty minutes. Drain and leave aside.
2. Wash and cut brinjals into one inch sized cubes and leave in water with a pinch of salt in it.
3. Wash and cut *tendli* lengthwise into four. Wash and chop fresh coriander leaves. Wash and remove stems from red chillies.
4. Dry roast coriander seeds, grated dry coconut, red chillies and cumin seeds separately and then grind to a fine paste.
5. Heat oil in a wide-mouthed *handi*. Add cloves, cardamoms, bay leaves and stir-fry for a few seconds.
6. Add ground *masala*, cook it for two to three minutes on medium heat, stirring continuously. Add vegetables and turmeric powder, cook further for three to four minutes.
7. Add rice and mix gently. Add three cups of boiling hot water. Season with salt.
8. Cook on high flame for five minutes, stirring frequently. Bring it to a boil and then reduce heat and continue to cook covered until rice is done and all the water is absorbed.
9. Remove from fire and serve hot, garnished with cashewnuts, chopped fresh coriander leaves and scraped coconut.

Chef's Tip: *For special occasions, you may prepare* masale bhaat *with basmati rice.*

INGREDIENTS

Ingredient	Quantity
Dry whole red chillies	20-25
Garlic	12-16 cloves
Ginger	1 one inch piece
Oil	2 tblspns
Lemon juice	1 tblspn
Vinegar	4 tblspns
Salt	to taste
Sugar	½ tspn

METHOD OF PREPARATION

1. Clean and remove the stems of red chillies. Peel and roughly chop garlic and ginger.
2. Heat oil in a pan, add roughly chopped garlic and ginger.
3. Stir-fry briefly, add red chillies and continue stir-frying for half a minute more. Remove from heat and cool.
4. Grind the above mixture with lemon juice, vinegar, salt and sugar to a fine paste.

INGREDIENTS

Basmati rice	2 cups	Mint leaves	12-15
Prawns	12-16 medium sized	Fresh coconut, scraped	½ cup
Lemon juice	1 tspn	Oil	3 tblspns
Salt	to taste	Cinnamon	1 one inch stick
Onions	2 medium sized	Black cardamoms	4
Green chillies	3	Star anise	2
Garlic	6-7 cloves	Cloves	4
Ginger	1 inch piece	Cumin seeds	1 tspn
Fresh coriander leaves	½ cup	Coconut milk	½ cup

METHOD OF PREPARATION

1. Clean *basmati* rice, wash two to three times with plenty of water. Soak in water for thirty minutes. Drain and keep aside.
2. Shell, devein and wash the prawns, marinate with lemon juice and salt.
3. Peel and finely chop the onions. Wash and remove the stems of green chillies. Wash and peel garlic and ginger. Wash fresh coriander leaves and mint leaves.
4. Reserve one tablespoon each of coriander leaves and scraped coconut for garnish.
5. Grind green chillies, mint, ginger, garlic and remaining fresh coriander leaves and coconut to a fine paste.
6. Heat oil in a thick-bottomed *handi*. Add cinnamon, black cardamoms, star anise, cloves and cumin seeds, sauté briefly.
7. Add chopped onions, sauté for three to four minutes or till they turn light golden-brown in colour. Add ground *masala* paste, stir-fry briefly and add the prawns. Sauté for two to three minutes.
8. Add soaked rice, stir gently for a minute. Stir in coconut milk.
9. Add four cups of hot water. Bring it to a boil, stirring once or twice. Cook on medium heat till water has almost evaporated. Reduce heat and cook covered till rice is done.
10. Remove from fire and serve, garnished with chopped fresh coriander and scraped coconut.

INGREDIENTS

Whole wheat flour .... 1 cup
Salt .... to taste
Semolina (*Rava*) .... 3 tblspns
Red chilli powder .... 2 tspns
Turmeric powder .... ½ tspn
Ajwain .... 1 tspn
Oil .... 2 tblspns + for deep-frying

METHOD OF PREPARATION

1. Mix and sieve the whole wheat flour and salt.
2. Add semolina, red chilli powder, turmeric powder, *ajwain* and two tablespoons of oil. Mix well.
3. Add water, a little at a time and knead to make a semi-hard dough. Cover with a moist cloth for half an hour.
4. Divide the dough into twelve to sixteen equal portions. Shape them into round balls and roll out each portion into thin discs of three to four inches diameter.
5. Heat oil in a *kadai* and deep-fry the rolled out *puris* on both sides till light golden brown in colour and nicely puffed. Remove *puris* from oil to an absorbent kitchen towel and serve immediately.

Chef's Tip: *These puris can be eaten as an evening snack with some pickle or served as an accompaniment for lunch or dinner.*

INGREDIENTS

Cucumbers	3 medium sized
Green chillies	2
Fresh coriander leaves	½ cup
Peanuts, roasted and peeled	½ cup
Fresh coconut, scraped	⅓ cup
Lemon juice	1 tblspn
Sugar	1 tspn
Salt	to taste
For tempering	
Pure *ghee*	1 tblspn
Mustard seeds	½ tspn
Cumin seeds	¼ tspn

METHOD OF PREPARATION

1. Peel, halve, remove seeds and finely chop cucumbers.
2. Wash, remove stems and finely chop green chillies. Clean, wash and finely chop fresh coriander leaves. Crush roasted peanuts to a coarse powder.
3. Mix cucumbers with peanut powder, scraped coconut, chopped green chillies, lemon juice and sugar.
4. Heat *ghee* in a small pan, add mustard seeds and let them crackle. Add cumin seeds, stir-fry briefly and add this tempering to the cucumber mixture and mix well.
5. Mix salt and serve immediately, garnished with chopped fresh coriander leaves.

TAMARIND – GINGER PICKLE

INSTANT COOKED PICKLE

INGREDIENTS

Tamarind	4 lemon sized balls
Ginger	6 one inch pieces
Green chillies	10
Fenugreek seeds	1 tspn
Asafoetida powder	¼ tspn
Salt	to taste
Til oil	10 tblspns
Turmeric powder	¼ tspn
Mustard seeds	½ tspn
Dry whole red chillies	2
Jaggery	1 tspn

METHOD OF PREPARATION

1. Soak tamarind in two cups of warm water for half an hour, remove the pulp, strain and keep aside.
2. Scrub, wash and spread ginger on an absorbent kitchen towel to dry out and finely chop or grate. Wash, remove stems and cut green chillies into half centimetre sized pieces.
3. Dry roast the fenugreek seeds in a hot pan to golden brown, pound to powder and mix with the asafoetida powder and salt.
4. Heat four tablespoons oil in a pan, add ginger and chillies, sauté for about two minutes and add turmeric powder. Stir well and cook for a minute on low flame and remove.
5. Heat the remaining oil, temper with mustard seeds, red chillies and stir in the tamarind pulp.
6. Bring to a boil, add the mixture of powdered fenugreek, asafoetida powder and salt. Mix and add the jaggery. Simmer on medium heat for six to eight minutes or till the mixture is reduced by half.
7. Add the cooked green chillies and ginger. Cook for two to three minutes on high flame, stirring continuously. Check and adjust seasoning.
8. Cool and store in a sterilized bottle.

Chef's Tip: *This pickle has a short shelf life of about six to seven days only. Store in the refrigerator if you intend to keep it longer. With the above measurements you can make 250 grams of this pickle.*

INGREDIENTS

Lemons	15-18 medium sized	*Til* oil	6 tblspns
Ginger	4 one inch pieces	Mustard seeds	1 tspn
Green chillies	10-12	Turmeric powder	¼ tspn
Fenugreek seeds	1 tspn	Salt	to taste
Asafoetida powder	½ tspn		

METHOD OF PREPARATION

1. Wash and soak lemons in hot water for half an hour. Drain, wipe them dry and cut them into two. Remove seeds and cut each half into four to five pieces.
2. Wash, peel and finely chop ginger. Wash, remove stems and cut green chillies into half inch sized pieces.
3. Dry roast fenugreek seeds, cool, grind to a powder and mix with asafoetida powder.
4. Heat oil in a pan, add mustard seeds and stir-fry till they crackle. Add chopped ginger and green chillies, sauté for two minutes. Add lemon pieces, turmeric powder and salt. Reduce heat and cook for ten minutes, stirring frequently.
5. Sprinkle fenugreek and asafoetida powder. Stir well and remove from heat.
6. Cool, pour into sterilized bottles and store in the refrigerator. With the above measurements you can make 500 gms of the pickle.

PANCHRANGA PULAO

ASSORTED VEGETABLES COOKED WITH BASMATI RICE

INGREDIENTS

Basmati rice .... 2 cups
Capsicum .... 1 medium sized
French beans 6-8
Carrot .... 1 medium sized
Cauliflower .... 8-10 small florets
Onions .... 2 medium sized
Pure *ghee* .... 3 tblspns
Cumin seeds .... 1 tspn
Cinnamon .... 1 one inch stick
Green cardamoms 3-4
Cloves 3-4
Black peppercorns .... 1 tblspn
Bay leaves 2
Green peas, shelled .... ¼ cup
Salt .... to taste

METHOD OF PREPARATION

1. Clean, wash and soak the rice for half an hour. Wash, halve, remove seeds and cut capsicum into half inch sized pieces. Wash, string and cut French beans into half inch sized pieces. Wash, peel and cut carrot into half inch sized pieces.
2. Wash and soak cauliflower in warm salted water for five minutes and drain. Peel and finely slice onion.
3. Heat pure *ghee* in a thick-bottomed pan and add cumin seeds, cinnamon, green cardamoms, cloves, peppercorns and bay leaves. Stir-fry briefly.
4. Add sliced onion and sauté for two to three minutes until the onion is translucent. Add cut carrots, French beans, cauliflower and green peas and cook for a minute.
5. Drain and add the soaked rice and stir-fry for a minute. Stir in four cups water and salt to taste. Bring to a boil and cook on medium heat for three to four minutes, stirring occasionally or until all the water is absorbed.
6. Stir in capsicum, reduce heat and cook covered for six to eight minutes or till rice and vegetables are cooked.
7. Remove from heat and keep it aside for five minutes before serving hot.

Panchranga Pulao

Khamang Kakdi, Varadhi Thetcha, Methamba

INGREDIENTS

Raw mangoes	3-4 medium sized
Salt	to taste
Dry whole red chillies	5-6
Cloves	6-8
Cinnamon	2 one inch sticks
Oil	1 cup
Mustard seeds	1 tspn
Asafoetida powder	¼ tspn
Fenugreek seeds	½ tspn
Jaggery, grated	2 ¼ cups

METHOD OF PREPARATION

1. Wash and wipe dry raw mangoes. Peel and cut them into halves. Remove seeds and cut into one inch sized pieces.
2. Apply salt and set aside for twenty-four hours. Wash the mango pieces and wipe them completely dry.
3. Clean and remove stems from red chillies. Grind cloves and cinnamon to a coarse powder.
4. Heat oil in a pan, add mustard seeds and once they start crackling add asafoetida powder, fenugreek seeds and red chillies. Stir-fry briefly.
5. Add mango pieces and jaggery. Cook on medium heat for five to six minutes or till jaggery melts completely and coats mango pieces. Remove from heat and sprinkle coarsely ground cloves and cinnamon.
6. Mix thoroughly and store *methamba* in a sterilized airtight bottle.

INGREDIENTS

Ladies' fingers	15-20	Mustard seeds	½ tspn
Oil	to deep-fry	Fenugreek seeds	¼ tspn
Yogurt	2 cups	Dry whole red chillies	2
Salt	to taste	Curry leaves	10-12
Asafoetida powder	¼ tspn		
Tempering			
Til oil	1 tblspn		

METHOD OF PREPARATION

1. Wipe, and finely slice the ladies' fingers and spread them out on an absorbent paper for about ten minutes. Heat oil in a *kadai* and deep-fry the ladies' fingers till crisp. Transfer them to an absorbent paper.
2. Whisk yogurt and add a little water if it is too thick. Mix salt and asafoetida powder in it. Stir in fried ladies' fingers.
3. Heat *til* oil and add mustard seeds; when they start crackling, add fenugreek seeds, red chillies and curry leaves. Pour the tempering on the *pachidi* and mix immediately to trap the flavours.

Chef's Tip: *Grind quarter cup scraped coconut and mix with the* pachidi *for variety. You can also make this with spinach.*

INGREDIENTS

Raw mangoes	12 medium sized	Salt	1½ cups
Mustard seeds	1 cup	Asafoetida powder	¼ tspn
Red chilli powder	2 cups	Fenugreek seeds	4 tblspns
Turmeric powder	¼ cup	*Til* oil	2 cups

METHOD OF PREPARATION

1. Select good, firm and sour mangoes. Wash thoroughly and wipe them completely dry with an absorbent kitchen towel .
2. Cut the mangoes into half with the seed and then cut each half into six to eight equal sized pieces. Spread them on a mat and dry in the sun for about two days.
3. Clean and dry the mustard seeds and pound to a coarse powder.
4. Thoroughly mix red chilli powder, turmeric powder, salt, asafoetida powder, mustard powder, fenugreek seeds and oil. Remove seeds from the sun-dried mango pieces and mix them with the pickle mixture.
5. Transfer to a ceramic pickle jar, tie the mouth with a muslin cloth and keep in the sun for three days without stirring.
6. Fourth day onwards, stir the pickle well and continue to keep in the sun for at least a week to ten days.
7. This pickle will last for a year if kept well.

Chef's Tip: *Use only good quality white* til *oil for the pickle. Freshly pounded or milled chilli powder is recommended. You may also add chick peas* (kabuli chana) *to this pickle.*

INGREDIENTS

Fresh coconut	½	Lemon juice	½ tblspn
Garlic	3-4 cloves	Sugar	2 tspns
Fresh coriander leaves	½ cup	Salt	to taste
Green chillies	3	Yogurt	3 tspns

METHOD OF PREPARATION

1. Scrape, grate or cut fresh coconut into small pieces. Peel and roughly chop garlic.
2. Clean, wash and roughly chop fresh coriander leaves. Wash, remove stems from green chillies and roughly chop.
3. Mix all the ingredients except yogurt and grind to a coarse paste in a mixer.
4. Mix yogurt in the *chutney* thoroughly, adjust seasoning and serve with snacks.

INGREDIENTS

Chana dal	1 cup	Coriander seeds	2 tblspns
Onion	1 medium sized	Cumin seeds	1 tspn
Garlic	6 cloves	Peppercorns	1 tblspn
Til oil	8 tblspns	Tamarind	½ lemon sized ball
Mustard seeds	½ tspn	Asafoetida powder	¼ tspn
Dry whole red chillies	6	Salt	to taste

METHOD OF PREPARATION

1. Clean, wash and soak *dal* for half an hour. Peel and finely slice the onion and garlic.
2. Heat oil in a pan, add mustard seeds and stir-fry for fifteen seconds. Add red chillies, coriander seeds, cumin seeds and peppercorns and sauté for two minutes. Add sliced onion and garlic and continue cooking on medium heat for two to three minutes.
3. Drain and add the soaked *chana dal* and tamarind; stir-fry on high heat for two to three minutes. Mix in asafoetida powder and salt.
4. Remove from fire and cool on a large flat plate. Grind to a coarse paste, adding a little water as required.

Chef's Tip: *You can use this as a sandwich spread or mix with little butter and serve it on a canapé. Try the same recipe with peanuts instead of the* dal. *With the above measurements you can make 500 gms of the* chutney.

INGREDIENTS

Urad dal, skinless .... ¾ cup
Turmeric powder .... ¼ tspn
Kokam .... 4-5 pieces
Goda masala .... 2 tspns
Salt .... to taste

For tempering

Green chillies 2
Garlic .... 4-5 cloves
Oil .... 2 tblspns
Mustard seeds .... ¼ tspn
Asafoetida powder .... ¼ tspn

METHOD OF PREPARATION

1. Wash, remove stems and finely chop the green chillies. Peel and finely chop garlic.
2. Clean, wash and soak *urad dal* in water for thirty minutes.
3. Drain and cook *urad dal* with three cups of water and turmeric powder till almost done.
4. Add *kokam, goda masala* and salt. Cook further on medium heat for five to six minutes, stirring occasionally or till *dal* is completely done.
5. Heat oil in a pan, add mustard seeds and let them crackle. Add chopped garlic and stir-fry till light golden brown.
6. Add chopped green chillies, asafoetida powder and sauté briefly. Temper the cooked *dal* with this mixture. Cover immediately with a lid to trap the aroma and leave aside for a couple of minutes.
7. Mix well and serve hot with steamed rice.

INGREDIENTS

Onions .... 4 medium sized
Garlic .... 8-10 cloves
Dry whole red chillies 4-5
Groundnut oil .... 3 tblspns
Roasted peanuts, skinless .... 1 cup
Tamarind .... ½ lemon sized ball
Asafoetida powder .... ¼ tspn
Salt .... to taste

METHOD OF PREPARATION

1. Peel and roughly chop onions and garlic. Clean and remove stems from red chillies.
2. Heat oil in a pan, add chopped onions and garlic; sauté for four to five minutes or until it turns golden brown in colour.
3. Add roasted peanuts, red chillies, tamarind, asafoetida powder and salt to taste. Stir well and cook for one minute. Remove from heat and cool to room temperature.
4. Grind this mixture to a slightly coarse *chutney*, adding a little water.
5. Store in the refrigerator and serve as an accompaniment.

INGREDIENTS

Refined flour (*Maida*) ......2 cups
Cooking soda ...... ¼ tspn
Salt ...... to taste
Yogurt ...... 2 tblspns
Milk ...... 2 tblspns
Oil ...... 3 tblspns
Potatoes ...... 2 medium sized
Onion ...... ½ medium sized
Fresh coriander leaves ...... ¼ cup
Mint leaves 8-10
Green chillies 2
Pomegranate seeds (*Anardana*) ...... 1 tspn
Red chilli powder ...... ½ tblspn
Cumin powder ...... 1 tblspn
Salt ...... to taste
Nigella seeds (*Kalonji*) ...... ¾ tspn
Butter ...... 2 tblspns

METHOD OF PREPARATION

1. Sieve refined flour with cooking soda and salt. Gradually mix in the yogurt and milk. Add sufficient water to make soft and smooth dough. Cover with a wet cloth and keep the dough for ten minutes.
2. Add two tablespoons oil and knead the dough well. Cover it once again and keep aside for at least an hour. Divide the dough into six to eight equal portions and form them into smooth balls.
3. Meanwhile, wash and boil potatoes. Cool, peel and grate them. Peel and finely chop the onion. Clean, wash and finely chop the fresh coriander leaves, mint leaves and green chillies.
4. Dry roast pomegranate seeds and grind to a coarse powder.
5. Mix boiled grated potatoes, chopped onion, fresh coriander leaves, mint leaves, green chillies, pomegranate seed powder, red chilli powder, cumin powder and salt to taste.
6. Divide the potato mixture into six to eight equal portions and keep aside.
7. Flatten a portion of the dough, place a portion of the potato mixture in the centre and fold the dough to form a ball.
8. Place the stuffed dough on a lightly floured surface and roll gently into a disc of four to five inch diameter. Brush lightly with oil. Sprinkle nigella seeds on the surface and press with your palm.
9. Place on a greased baking tray and bake in a preheated oven at 220 degrees Celsius for about six to eight minutes.
10. Brush the hot *kulcha* with butter and serve immediately.

Chef's Tip: *Traditionally this* kulcha *is cooked in the tandoor. This dish was one of the hot selling items in my restaurant in New Zealand, not as an accompaniment but as a starter.*

Modak, Rava Naral Laddu

Mysore Pak, Sweet Pongal

INGREDIENTS

Cornmeal (*Makai ka atta*) .... 1½ cups
Whole wheat flour (optional) ...... ¼ cup
Salt .... to taste
Butter .... 6 tblspns

METHOD OF PREPARATION

1. Mix cornmeal, whole wheat flour and salt. Add sufficient lukewarm water, a little at a time to make a medium-soft dough.
2. Divide the prepared dough into eight to ten equal portions. Moisten your palm with a little water and flatten each portion of the dough on a wet polythene sheet into discs of four to five inches diameter.
3. Heat a *tawa*, apply a little oil and transfer *makki roti* carefully to the *tawa*. Spoon a little oil on the sides of *makki roti* and cook on low heat for one minute.
4. Turn the *makki roti* and cook the other side for one minute or till crisp and light golden brown.
5. Brush the cooked *rotis* with butter and serve hot with *sarson ka saag*.

DHAABAY DI DAL

DAL AS COOKED IN A ROAD-SIDE EATERY

INGREDIENTS

Urad dal, with skin	½ cup
Chana dal	¼ cup
Red kidney beans	¼ cup
Onions	2 medium sized
Garlic	8-10 cloves
Green chillies	2-3
Tomatoes	3 medium sized
Oil	4 tblspns
Red chilli powder	1 tblspn
Cumin powder	1 tblspn
Butter	3 tblspns
Salt	to taste
Fresh coriander leaves	¼ cup
Kasuri methi	1 tblspn

METHOD OF PREPARATION

1. Clean, wash and soak *urad dal*, *chana dal* and kidney beans in sufficient water for at least six hours.
2. Peel and finely chop onions and garlic. Wash, remove stems and finely chop green chillies. Wash and finely chop tomatoes.
3. Drain soaked *dals*, add six cups of water and pressure-cook for half an hour or until the *dals* are completely cooked.
4. Meanwhile, heat oil in a pan, add chopped garlic, stir-fry briefly till golden brown. Add chopped onion, slit green chillies and sauté for four to five minutes or until the onion is golden brown in colour.
5. Add red chilli powder, cumin powder and stir-fry briefly. Add chopped tomatoes and cook on high heat for three to four minutes, stirring continuously. Stir in the cooked *dals* and butter and mix well.
6. Add salt, chopped coriander leaves and cook *dal* for ten minutes on low heat, stirring occasionally.
7. Crush *kasuri methi* between the palms, sprinkle on the *dal* and serve hot.

INGREDIENTS

Chana dal .... 1 cup
Potatoes .... 2 medium sized
Ginger .... 2 one inch pieces
Green chillies 2
Fresh coriander leaves .... a few sprigs
Fresh coconut, scraped .... ½ cup
Salt .... to taste
Oil .... 3 tblspns + for frying
Coriander powder .... 3 tblspns
Cumin powder .... 1 ½ tspns
Red chilli powder .... 1 ½ tspns
Turmeric powder .... ½ tspn
Garam masala powder .... 1 tspn

METHOD OF PREPARATION

1 Clean, wash and soak *chana dal* for six to eight hours. Drain and grind to a fine paste.
2 Wash, peel and slice potatoes into quarter centimetre thick roundels. Keep them in water till required.
3 Peel ginger and grind to a fine paste. Wash, remove stems and slit green chillies. Clean, wash and finely chop fresh coriander leaves.
4 Mix ground *chana dal*, scraped coconut and salt to taste. Pour the mixture into a greased plate that is at least one and half inches deep or a tray measuring approximately 6 x 6 x 1 ½ inches.
5 Steam on high heat for fifteen to twenty minutes or till firm and cooked. Check by inserting a skewer into the cooked mixture and if it comes out clean, then it is cooked. Remove, cool a little and cut into one inch sized cubes or into diamond shaped pieces.
6 Heat oil in a *kadai* and deep-fry the pieces till they turn light golden. Drain on a clean absorbent kitchen towel or paper and keep aside.
7 Drain and pat dry potato roundels and deep fry in the same oil for a minute. Drain on a clean absorbent kitchen towel or paper and keep aside.
8 Heat three tablespoons oil and add green chillies and ginger paste. Stir-fry briefly and immediately add coriander powder, cumin powder, red chilli powder and turmeric powder. Mix well.
9 Add quarter cup water. Reduce heat and continue cooking on medium heat for three to four minutes. Add potato roundels and cook for another two minutes, stirring occasionally.
10 Stir in two cups of water and bring to a boil. Add fried *chana dal* pieces, reduce heat and simmer for five minutes.
11 Add *garam masala* and serve hot, garnished with chopped fresh coriander leaves.

SWEET PONGAL

RICE AND MOONG COOKED WITH JAGGERY

INGREDIENTS

Rice	1½ cups
Moong dal	½ cup
Cardamoms	4
Sugar	1 tblspn
Jaggery	2 cups
Milk	2 ½ cups
Pure *ghee*	½ cup
Fresh coconut, scraped	½ cup
Nutmeg, grated	¼ tspn
Raisins	4 tblspns
Cashewnuts	12-15
Edible camphor (optional)	1 pinch

METHOD OF PREPARATION

1. Clean, wash and soak the rice for half an hour. Dry roast the *moong dal* lightly in a hot *kadai*.
2. Grind cardamoms with sugar to a fine powder, sieve and keep aside.
3. Break the jaggery into very small pieces and keep. Boil milk with one cup water in a thick-bottomed pan.
4. Wash and drain the *dal* and the rice, add to the boiling milk. Bring to a boil, stirring continuously. Reduce heat, simmer for fifteen minutes, stirring occasionally or till rice and *dal* are completely cooked. You can also pressure cook it.
5. Add jaggery and keep stirring to prevent it from sticking to the bottom. Keep cooking till all the jaggery melts completely and is thoroughly incorporated in the rice and *dal* mixture. Add half the quantity of *ghee* and continue cooking on low heat for about five minutes, stirring frequently.
6. Heat the remaining pure *ghee* separately and fry the scraped coconut lightly. Add grated nutmeg, raisins and cashewnuts and stir well. Add this to the cooked *pongal*.
7. Sprinkle the cardamom powder and the camphor powder. Stir well and serve hot.

***Chef's Tip:** You can use sugar or even palm jaggery for making the* pongal. *Add coconut milk instead of scraped coconut for a richer taste.*

INGREDIENTS

Gram flour (*Besan*) .... ¾ cup   Sugar .... 4 cups
Pure ghee .... 2½ cups

METHOD OF PREPARATION

1. Break lumps and sieve gram flour twice. Preheat the pure *ghee* and keep it hot.
2. Cook sugar with half a litre of water on medium heat, stirring continuously till it dissolves. Increase heat and bring syrup to a boil. Cook without stirring for about five minutes or till it reaches single thread consistency.
3. Add half a cup of hot pure *ghee* to the syrup and stir, add gram flour gradually stirring all the while to prevent any lump formation.
4. Keep on stirring continuously till the mixture starts bubbling.
5. Add the hot *ghee,* half a cup at a time. Every time you add the *ghee* it should sizzle and froth up.
6. Continue this process till all the *ghee* is used up and you get a pleasant sweet and a roasted gram flour aroma.
7. Pour this on a greased tray. Cool a little and cut into desired shape.

Chef's Tip: *We recommend using of pure* ghee *but it can be substituted with* vanaspati. *Store in an airtight container to retain the freshness and crispness. With the above measurements you can make around forty to forty-five* barfis.

INGREDIENTS

Pistachio nuts	8-10	*Paneer*, freshly made	400 gms
Almonds	10-12	Sugar, powdered	½ cup
Saffron	a generous pinch	Cardamom powder	½ tspn
Warm milk	1 tblspn		

METHOD OF PREPARATION

1. Soak pistachio nuts and almonds in one cup water for ten minutes. Drain, peel and chop pistachio nuts and almonds. Lightly crush and dissolve saffron in warm milk. Mix chopped pistachio nuts in milk and saffron mixture.
2. Knead *paneer* with your palm to ensure that it is quite smooth in texture. Add powdered sugar and cardamom powder and knead well.
3. Transfer the mixture to a *kadai* and cook on low flame for five to six minutes, stirring continuously. Remove from fire, mix gently till it is cool enough to handle.
4. Mix in chopped almonds and divide into twenty equal portions.
5. Form each portion into desired shape, garnish with chopped pistachio nuts and soaked saffron. Chill thoroughly and serve.

Chef's Tip: *Since* sandesh *has short life, it is recommended that it should be consumed on the same day.*

INGREDIENTS

Carrots	8-10 medium sized	Green cardamom powder	½ tspn
Raisins	2 tblspns	*Khoya*, grated	1 cup
Pure *ghee*	¼ cup	Sugar	1 cup
Milk	1 cup	Cashewnuts	8-10

METHOD OF PREPARATION

1. Wash, peel and grate carrots. Wash and pat dry raisins.
2. Heat pure *ghee* in a thick-bottomed pan, add grated carrots and sauté for five minutes. Add milk, green cardamom powder and cook on medium heat for five to six minutes or until the milk evaporates and the carrots are cooked.
3. Stir in the grated *khoya* and sugar and cook for two to three minutes or till the sugar melts and mixes well, stirring continuously.
4. Add raisins and cashewnuts and continue to cook for two minutes more and serve hot or at room temperature.

KESARI RAJBHOG

STUFFED BENGALI SWEET

INGREDIENTS

Paneer, from cow's milk	250 gms	*Khoya,* grated	3 tblspns
Refined flour (*Maida*)	1 tspn	Green cardamom powder	½ tspn
Semolina (*Rava*)	1 tspn	Rose syrup	2 tspns
Pistachio nuts	12-15	Sugar	4-5 cups
Almonds	6-8	Saffron *(Kesar)*	½ tspn

METHOD OF PREPARATION

1. Take fresh *paneer*, knead it well until smooth.
2. Add refined flour and semolina and then knead it gently. Divide into twelve to fourteen equal portions.
3. Soak pistachio nuts and almonds in one cup boiling water for five minutes. Drain, cool, peel and chop them roughly.
4. Combine grated *khoya* with green cardamom powder and rose syrup. Knead it into dough. Mix in the roughly chopped pistachio nuts and almonds; divide into twelve to fourteen equal portions.
5. Stuff a portion of *khoya* into each portion of *paneer* and make marble-sized balls.
6. Combine sugar with three-fourth litre water. Bring it to a boil and make thin sugar syrup. Remove scum, if any and pass it through a muslin cloth.
7. Bring sugar syrup to a boil in a wide-mouthed pan and add saffron. Gently slide in stuffed *paneer* balls and cook for four to five minutes on high heat.
8. Sprinkle about quarter cup hot water and continue to cook on high heat for another five minutes or till they are almost double in size. Remove and keep in sufficient quantity of saffron infused sugar syrup.
9. Refrigerate and serve chilled.

Gajar Halwa, Strawberry Phirni

Sandesh, Kesari Rajbhog

INGREDIENTS

Rice	4 tblspns	Milk	1 litre
Fresh Strawberries	12-15	Sugar	¾ cup
Pistachio nuts	8-10	Green cardamom powder	½ tspn
Almonds	6-8		

METHOD OF PREPARATION

1. Clean, wash and soak rice in sufficient water for half an hour. Drain and grind the soaked rice to a coarse paste. Dilute rice paste with half cup of water. Wash, hull and slice two strawberries and finely chop the remaining.
2. Soak pistachio nuts and almonds in hot water for five minutes, drain, peel and finely slice.
3. Heat milk and bring to a boil. Gradually stir in the rice paste, reduce heat and simmer for three to four minutes, stirring continuously or till the milk is well thickened.
4. Add sugar, cardamom powder and continue to simmer till sugar dissolves and mixes well. Remove from heat, cool to room temperature and stir in the chopped strawberries.
5. Pour this mixture into earthenware or ceramic bowls, garnish with sliced pistachio nuts, almonds and sliced strawberries and serve chilled.

INGREDIENTS

Pure *ghee*	4 tblspns	Sugar	1½ cups
Vermicelli	1 cup	Saffron	a generous pinch
Cashewnuts	8-10	Green cardamom powder	½ tspn
Milk	4 cups	Nutmeg, grated	a pinch

METHOD OF PREPARATION

1. Heat pure *ghee* in a pan, add vermicelli and sauté for two to three minutes or until light golden brown in colour. Add cashewnuts, stir well and keep aside.
2. Heat milk in a thick bottomed pan, bring to a boil, and add the sautéed vermicelli and cashewnuts. Mix gently, reduce heat and simmer for five minutes, stirring frequently.
3. Add sugar and continue to simmer, stirring frequently. Cook for three to four minutes or until the *payasam* has thickened well.
4. Stir in saffron, green cardamom powder and grated nutmeg. Mix well and serve hot, chilled or at room temperature.

INGREDIENTS

Yogurt	3 cups	Saffron	a generous pinch
Powdered sugar	2 ½ cups	Warm milk	2 tblspns
Pistachio nuts	8-10	Green cardamom powder	¼ tspn
Chironji	2 tspns		

METHOD OF PREPARATION

1. Tie yogurt in a muslin cloth and hang it overnight, to drain out the whey. This should preferably be hung in the refrigerator.
2. Transfer the hung yogurt into a bowl. Add powdered sugar and mix well till sugar dissolves completely.
3. Soak pistachio nuts in hot water for five to ten minutes. Drain, peel and slice them. Clean, wash and pat dry *chironji*.
4. Dissolve saffron in a little warm milk and add to the yogurt mixture. Mix well.
5. Add *chironji* and green cardamom powder and mix well. Serve chilled, garnished with sliced pistachio nuts.

Chef's Tip: *Add one cup mango puree to this* shrikhand *to make* amrakhand, *best enjoyed during summers.*

124

ADA PRADHAMAN

DRIED RICE CAKE COOKED WITH COCONUT MILK AND PALM JAGGERY

INGREDIENTS

Pure *ghee*	¼ cup	Cashewnuts	12
Ada	1 cup	Raisins	2 tblspns
Green cardamoms	4	Fresh coconut, scraped	1½ cups
Sugar	1 tblspn	Palm jaggery	200 gms

METHOD OF PREPARATION

1. Heat two tablespoons *ghee* and fry the *ada* lightly.
2. Grind the cardamoms with the sugar to a fine powder, sieve and keep aside. Heat two tablespoons *ghee* and fry cashewnuts and raisins till light brown.
3. Soak the scraped coconut in one cup warm water, grind and extract thick milk. Repeat the process and make a second extract and keep aside. Break the jaggery into smaller pieces.
4. Cook the fried *ada* in one cup boiling water and the second extract of coconut milk, till it is soft but holds its shape.
5. Add the jaggery and continue cooking till it thickens. Heat the remaining *ghee* and add to the cooked *ada*.
6. Add the first extract of coconut milk, stir and mix the fried cashewnuts and raisins. Stir well and heat through without boiling the mixture.
7. Sprinkle the cardamom powder and serve at room temperature.

METHOD OF PREPARING ADA

Soak three quarter cup raw rice for about one hour in sufficient water, wash and drain well. Dry the soaked rice on a sheet of dry, absorbent cloth for twenty minutes and grind to a fine powder. Sieve and mix with one cup warm water to make a thick paste. Spread this batter on a piece of banana leaf, roll and tie with a string. Steam the rolls for fifteen minutes on high heat and cool. Peel the *ada* from the leaves and cut into small discs. Dry overnight and use. If you want to store them for future use then dry well under hot sun and keep in an airtight container.

Chef's Tip: *Normally, readymade* ada *is available at any shop specializing in South Indian items.*

INGREDIENTS

Parboiled rice .... 1 ½ cups
Salt .... a pinch
Pure *ghee* .... ½ tspn

For stuffing

Fresh coconut, scraped .... 1 ½ cups
Jaggery, grated .... ¾ cup
Green cardamom powder ..... a pinch

METHOD OF PREPARATION

1. Clean, wash and drain rice thoroughly. Dry completely by spreading on an absorbent sheet of cloth. Grind dried rice to a fine powder. Pass it through a fine sieve.
2. Bring one and a quarter cups water to a boil in a pan; add salt and *ghee* to it.
3. Add rice flour in a flow, stirring continuously to prevent lumps from forming. Remove the pan from heat and keep it covered for ten to fifteen minutes.
4. Grease your palms with a little oil and knead the cooked rice mixture to a soft dough. Keep covered with a moist cloth.
5. Combine scraped coconut and jaggery in a pan and cook on medium heat for one or two minutes or till light golden brown. Ensure that it is not overcooked. Add green cardamom powder and remove from heat and cool it slightly. Divide the coconut mixture into ten to twelve equal sized portions.
6. Divide the dough into ten to twelve lemon sized balls. With greased palms flatten each ball to form discs with a diameter of three inches. Press the edges of the disc further to reduce the thickness.
7. Place a portion of coconut and jaggery mixture in the centre, form eight to ten pleats with fingers, gather them together to form a bundle and seal the edges at the top.
8. Steam them in an *idli* steamer for ten to twelve minutes. Serve hot *modak* with pure *ghee*.

KHAJOORI SHAHI TUKRA

ROYAL DATE AND BREAD DESSERT

INGREDIENTS

Bread	8 slices	Green cardamom powder	½ tspn
Pure *ghee*	for frying	Milk	5 cups
Pistachio nuts	10-12	Sugar	½ cup
Almonds	8-10	Silver *varq*	for garnish
Dates, seedless	1 cup	Rose water	½ tspn

METHOD OF PREPARATION

1. Trim the crust and cut each bread slice into a round shape with a cookie cutter or a *katori*. Heat pure *ghee* in a pan and shallow-fry the bread pieces for about a minute, turn over and fry for a minute more or until they turn light brown and crisp. Drain and keep on an absorbent kitchen towel or paper.
2. Soak pistachio nuts and almonds in hot water for ten minutes, drain, peel and slice. Reserve one tablespoon of sliced pistachio nuts and almonds for garnish.
3. Finely chop seedless dates, add green cardamom powder and mash thoroughly with a rolling pin. Add the sliced pistachio nuts and almonds and mix well. Divide this mixture into four equal portions.
4. Press a portion of the date mixture on a fried bread piece; cover with another fried bread piece and press to secure.
5. Meanwhile, bring milk to boil, reduce heat and simmer for ten minutes, stirring continuously or till the quantity is reduced to half. Add sugar and continue to simmer for five minutes, stirring continuously.
6. Dip date stuffed bread pieces in this mixture for half a minute, remove and keep aside. Cook the remaining milk for five to six minutes, stirring continuously or till it thickens to a coating consistency. Remove from heat and chill.
7. Place soaked bread pieces on a serving dish, pour chilled milk on top, apply silver *varq*, and top with reserved pistachio nuts and almonds. Serve sprinkled with rose syrup.

INGREDIENTS

Pure ghee	4 tblspns	Sugar	1 cup
Semolina (*Rava*)	1 ½ cups	Raisins	2 tblspns
Fresh coconut, scraped	¾ cup	Green cardamom powder	½ tspn

METHOD OF PREPARATION

1. Heat *ghee* in a thick-bottomed *kadai*, stir-fry semolina on a very low flame, till it just starts changing colour to light golden. Add scraped coconut and continue to stir-fry for one more minute.
2. Cook sugar with half a cup of water on medium heat, stirring continuously till it dissolves. Increase heat and bring the syrup to a boil. Cook without stirring for about five minutes or till it reaches single thread consistency.
3. Add the warm roasted semolina mixture and green cardamom powder to the sugar syrup and mix well. Cover the mixture with a lid and keep aside for thirty minutes, stirring the mixture at regular intervals.
4. Divide the mixture into twelve to fifteen equal portions, shape into firm *laddus* by rolling them with your hands and decorate with raisins.

INGREDIENTS

Pure ghee	4 tblspns	Sugar	1 cup
Semolina (*Rava*)	1 ½ cups	Raisins	2 tblspns
Fresh coconut, scraped	¾ cup	Green cardamom powder	½ tspn

METHOD OF PREPARATION

1. Heat *ghee* in a thick-bottomed *kadai*, stir-fry semolina on a very low flame, till it just starts changing colour to light golden. Add scraped coconut and continue to stir-fry for one more minute.
2. Cook sugar with half a cup of water on medium heat, stirring continuously till it dissolves. Increase heat and bring the syrup to a boil. Cook without stirring for about five minutes or till it reaches single thread consistency.
3. Add the warm roasted semolina mixture and green cardamom powder to the sugar syrup and mix well. Cover the mixture with a lid and keep aside for thirty minutes, stirring the mixture at regular intervals.
4. Divide the mixture into twelve to fifteen equal portions, shape into firm *laddus* by rolling them with your hands and decorate with raisins.

English	Hindi	
Ingredients		
Almond	Badam	Used as a garnish for sweets and as an ingredient in pulaos and curries.
Asafoetida	Hing	A powerful seasoning, used to flavour curries.
Bay leaves	Tej patta	These dried leaves are used to flavour curries and rice.
Black cardamom	Badi ilaichi	Used for flavouring curries and pulaos.
Black gram	Urad (whole)	Whole *urad* and *urad dal* are used to make curries. *Urad dal* is also used to make *dosa*, idli and *medu vada*, the famous South Indian snacks.
Black peppercorn	Kali mirch	This hot pungent spice is an important ingredient of *garam masala*. The pepper powder is often used in curries, rice and savoury dishes.
Bengal gram	Chana	This pulse and its *dal* are used to make curries
Bitter gourd	Karela	As the name suggests, this vegetable is bitter but makes tasty preparations
Black cumin seeds	Kala jira	This spice is used to flavour curries and pulaos especially in Norhern India.
Black salt	Kala namak	This salt adds its special flavour when added to *chaats* and to the water used while eating *pani puris*.
Bottle gourd	Lauki or doodhi	This is a watery vegetable, used in curries and at times in sweets.
Brinjal	Baingan	A widely used vegetable, it is especially tasty when made into *bharta* or stuffed.
Cabbage	Bandh gobi	Used in vegetable dishes and also served raw in salads.
Capsicum	Simla mirch	A vegetable, it is used in salads and in curries.

Caraway seeds	Shahi jeera	Used for flavouring curries and pulaos.
Carom seeds	Ajwain	Also known as Bishop's weed. Used as a part of batters, *masalas* and in savoury dishes.
Carrot	Gajar	Used in curries, salads and also sweets.
Cashewnuts	Kaju	Used as a garnish or for decoration in pulaos, curries and sweets.
Cauliflower	Phool gobhi	Used in curries and pulaos.
Chick peas	Kabuli chana	Specially used in making *chholay*.
Chilli	Mirch	Green dry red chillies or red chilli powder are used extensively in Indian cooking to make the food pungent
Cinnamon	Dalchini	These dry sticks are used to flavour curries, pulaos and is an important ingredient of *garam masala*.
Cloves	Lavang	Used in both sweet and savoury dishes.
Coconut	Narial	An important part of South Indian cooking. The milk and flesh extracted from the coconut is used as a base for curries, soups, *chutneys*, sweets and as a garnish.
Coriander seeds	Dhania	Used whole and in the powdered form in curries and vegetables and as a part of *garam masala*.
Coriander leaves	Hara dhania	Used as a garnish in several dishes and snacks.
Corn	Makai	Used in some curries and snacks.
Cottage cheese	Paneer	Used in vegetables as well as a base in (Indian) sweet dishes, especially when made from cow's milk.
Cucumber	Kheera or kakri	Low calorie vegetable, used mostly in salads.

Cumin seeds	Jeera	Used whole or ground, it imparts a spicy, aromatic flavour to curries, pulaos and *raitas*. Light roasting in a dry pan enhances its aroma.
Curry leaves	Kadhi patta	Used fresh or dried, they have a warm, appetizing aroma and give a delicate spicy flavour to the dish. Used extensively in South Indian cooking.
Dates	Khajoor	In its dried form it is used in making sweet and sour *chutneys* and in sweets.
Dry mango powder	Amchur	Used in curries and vegetables to give sour and tangy taste.
Fennel seeds	Saunf	These dried seeds are used extensively to flavour curries and pickles. They have a sweet aromatic flavour.
Fenugreek leaves	Methi	Fresh leaves are used as a vegetable and in *paranthas*. Dried leaves, known as *kasuri methi* are used for seasoning curries.
Fenugreek seeds	Methi dana	Whole seeds are used for seasoning, whereas the powder is an essential ingredient of pickles. For best results, lightly roast.
French beans	Fransbean	Used in curries and pulaos.
Fresh cream (Home-made)	Malai	Used in sweets and some curries. Home-made *malai* can be obtained by letting boiled milk cool and skimming off the layer of fat that forms on the surface. Commercial fresh cream is fat collected by churning whole milk at high speed.
Garlic	Lehsun	Often used whole or in paste form, in combination with ginger, to flavour curries and pickles.
Ginger	Adrak	Used in chopped or in the paste form in curries and vegetables.

		In julienne form it is used as a garnish. Dried ginger root is sometimes used to flavour pickles.
Ginger powder	Saunth	This can be used in place of fresh ginger. Popular in Kashmiri food.
Gram flour	Besan	Ground gram/*chana dal* is used in many sweet and savoury dishes. It is also used for thickening or binding.
Green cardamom	Chhoti ilaichi	Used whole, as a part of *garam masala* and in the powdered form to flavour sweets and some rice dishes.
Green gram	Moong	Used as whole, or sprouted or split (*dal*). Skinless split gram (*moong dal, dhuli*) is used for making curries or sweets.
Green peas	Matar	These can be used fresh or frozen in curries or pulaos.
Groundnut	Moong phalli	Used raw or roasted in some curries specially in Maharashtrian and Gujarati dishes.
Honey	Shahad	Used as a sugar substitute.
Jackfruit	Kathal	Raw fruit is used in curries. Its *koftas* are especially delicious. Ripe ones are used to make certain Manglorean and Konkan sweet dishes.
Jaggery	Gud	A sugar substitute, it imparts a delicate earthy taste to the dish.
Ladies' fingers (*Okra*)	Bhindi	This is a gummy vegetable and should be cooked dry to get best results.
Lentil	Masoor	Used both as whole and in split form (*dal*) in curries.
Lime	Nimbu	A citrus fruit used to add sourness to salads. It also adds a distinct flavour.
Mace	Javantri/Javitri	It is the outer covering of nutmeg. It has a delicate flavour and is used as an ingredient in *masala*.

Mango	Aam	Needs no introduction. It is indeed the king of fruits.
Mint leaves	Pudina	These leaves are widely used in *Chutneys* and as a flavouring for yogurt and in appetizers. Dried leaves are ground to make mint powder.
Mushroom	Dhingri	Usually used in combination with green peas or fresh corn to make exotic dishes. It is added to pulaos too.
Mustard seeds	Rai/Sarson	Whole seeds are used for tempering and in powder or crushed form in pickles.
Nutmeg	Jaiphal	Its sweet, woody scent adds a special flavour to sweet dishes.
Onion	Piaz	Chopped or sliced or ground, it is used as a base in many curries and vegetables. Different gravies require different onion pastes. For instance, white gravies require boiled onion paste while red gravies use browned onion paste.
Nigella seeds	Kalonji	Dry wild onion seeds are used in pickles and as a topping for naans.
Papaya	Papita	Raw papaya paste is used as a meat tenderizer. Ripe papaya is used as a base for some jams.
Pigeon peas	Toor	These in their split form are used to make curries and *dals*.
Pineapple	Ananas	This strongly flavoured fruit is used in salads and some puddings and cakes.
Pistachio	Pista	Used to garnish quite a few sweets.
Plantain (Banana)	Kela	In its raw form it is used to make *koftas* or in some South Indian curries. In its ripe form it is the most commonly eaten fruit. It is also used to make some sweets.
Pomegranate seeds	Anardana	Used to add tanginess in curries especially in *chana* preparations.

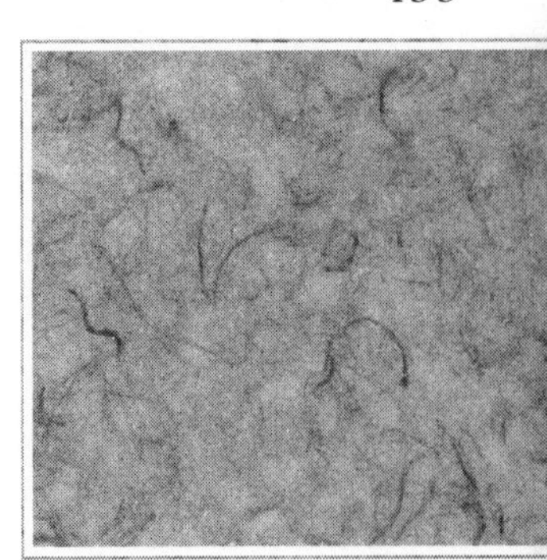

Poppy seeds	Khus khus	Used to thicken curries.
Potato	Aloo	Perhaps the most popular and commonly used vegetables the world over.
Pumpkin	Kaddu	Used in some curries and also to make a delightful *halwa*.
Radish	Mooli	Used mainly in salads, *mooli parathas* make a tasty breakfast item.
Raisins	Kishmish	Used as a garnish in many Indian sweets.
Refined flour	Maida	Used as a base to make different Indian breads and also to make snacks.
Ridge gourd	Turia	Green vegetable, as the name suggests it has ridges and is used in some curries.
Rose water	Gulab jal	Rose water and rose essence are especially used in Indian sweets like *gulab jamuns* and in *sherbets*.
Saffron	Kesar	This rare and expensive spice is used in minute quantities to flavour milk-based sweets and sometimes in special curries and *biryanis*. To get maximum flavour, saffron should be dissolved in warm milk for about twenty minutes before use.
Semolina	Suji/Rawa	Used to make Indian breads like *paranthas*, *puris* and as a base in some sweets.
Sesame seeds	Til	The seeds are used in some sweets. Roasted sesame paste is sometimes added to flavour and thicken the spicy curries. Sesame oil is used for cooking in some parts of the country. For better flavour, slightly roast the seeds until they jump.
Soda bicarbonate	Khanay ka soda	Used in fritters, etc.
Spinach	Palak	This leafy green vegetable is highly nutritious and is used in curries and soups.

Star anise	Badiyan/Phoolchakri	This dried, reddish-brown fruit, used in small quantities, gives a distinctive aroma to the dish.
Sweet potato	Shakarkand	This has a sweetish taste and can be fried, boiled, roasted or cooked in gravy.
Tamarind	Imli	Added to curries to give a mild, refreshing, sour taste. Tamarind pulp, which can be stored in the refrigerator, is used more often in curries and chutneys. When combined with sugar and other spices and mixed with cold water, it makes a delightfully cooling drink.
Turmeric	Haldi	The yellow coloured powder of the turmeric root gives a distinct flavour and colour to the curries, vegetables and pulaos. It also has medicinal properties and acts like an antibiotic.
Vinegar	Sirka	This liquid when added not only gives a sour taste, it also adds a distinct flavour. It is used mainly in Goan and Parsi cooking.
Walnut	Akhrot	This dry fruit is used as garnish and also as an ingredient in many Indian sweets.
Wheat flour	Atta	Whole meal flour is used as a base to make different Indian breads.
Yam	Jamikand/Sooran	Used widely in South Indian cooking, its *koftas* are quite tasty.
Yogurt/curd	Dahi	Yogurt is added to cooked dishes and also as a base for raitas, snacks like *dahi vada* and consumed in its liquid form as *lassi* or buttermilk.

Some Indian terms

Bharwan	Stuffed.
Biryani	Rice dish cooked in layers with spicy mutton, chicken or vegetables usually on special occasions.

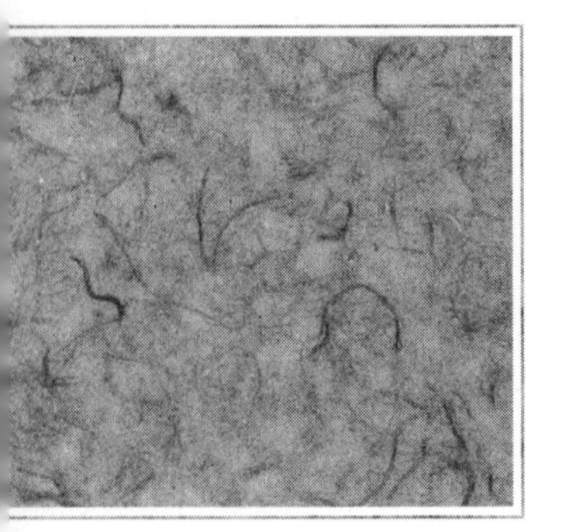

Chironji	Also known as *charoli* seeds. Used as garnish in Indian sweets.
Chenna	A form of cottage cheese, used as a base for Bengali sweets like *rosogolla* or *rasmalai*.
Garam masala	Spice powder. Lightly roast and grind the following ingredients to make the *masala* : Black cardamoms 8-10, Green cardamoms 15-20, Cinnamons 15-20 pieces (1 inch each), Cloves 1 tblspn, Mace 1 flower, Nutmeg 1, Peppercorns 1 tblspn, Cumin seeds ½ cup, Coriander seeds 2 tblspns.
Ghee	Clarified butter. Used as a cooking medium in some dishes instead of oil.
Goda masala	Coriander seeds 1 kg, Cumin seeds 200 gms, Stone flower 50 gms, Cinnamons 50 gms, Cardamoms 50 gms, Cloves 25 gms, *Shahi jeera* 25 gms, Peppercorns 100 gms, Bay leaves 50 gms, *Nagkeshar* 25 gms, Mace 25 gms, Grated *khopra* 200 gms, Sesame seeds 75 gms, Dry red chillies 75 gms, Asafoetida powder 25 gms. Roast all the ingredients one by one in a little oil. Cool and powder.
Kodumpuli	Also called fish tamarind, has a smoky sourness and gives a special flavour to the fish preparations and is used extensively in the Malabar region. It can be substituted with regular tamarind also.
Kokam	This sour, dry red fruit, also known as *Amsool* or red mango, is used to add sourness. Widely used in the Konkan belt.
Kabab	Meats (like mutton, Chicken or fish) and some vegetables (like cauliflower), marinated,

skewered and cooked in a *tandoor*, grill or oven. Some kababs like *shammi kabab*, are shallow-fried.

Kheema — Minced mutton or chicken.

Kofta — Spicy mutton, chicken or vegetable balls deep-fried and served with gravy.

Malwani masala — Dry red chillies 1 kg, Coriander seeds ½ kg, cloves 20 gms, Peppercorns 50 gms, Fennel seeds 100 gms, Cumin seeds 25 gms: *Shahi jeera* 25 gms, Black cardamoms 50 gms, Cinnamon 50 gms, Stone flower 50 gms, *Nagkeshar* 25 gms, Mustard seeds 25 gms, Turmeric knobs 25 gms, Asafoetida powder 25 gms, Nutmeg 2, *Badalphool* 10 gms. Dry roast the ingredients separately, cool and powder.

Masala — Spice powders. Indian cooking uses different kinds of *masalas* such as *garam masala, goda masala, chaat masala, sambar masala*.

Mawa — *Khoya*. Used as a base for sweets and as a thickener in some curries.

Papad — Thin and spiced lentil discs usually fried or roasted and used as an accompaniment.

Pulao — Rice simmered with vegetables or mutton or chicken and spices.

Raita — Yoghurt mixed with chopped vegetables or *boondi* (deep-fried corn sized *besan* balls).

Tikki — Minced mutton or chicken or cooked mashed vegetables mixed with spices and cooked in a tandoor or oven.

Some Indian utensils

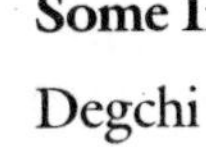

Degchi — A wide, thick-bottomed vessel.

Handi — A heavy-bottomed vessel, used to cook vegetables, curries, rice.

Kadai	A deep pan, mainly used for deep-frying.
Katori	A small bowl.
Patila	A large bowl, a thin-bottomed vessel.
Tandoor	A traditional clay oven fired by charcoal. Used for baking breads like *naan* and *tandoori roti* and for roasting meat, vegetables and *paneer*. The charcoal fire gives a smoked flavour to the dish.
Tawa	A thick, flat pan, used to make Indian breads, rotis, *paranthas*.
Tawi	A shallow frying pan, used for jalebis.
Thali	A metal plate.

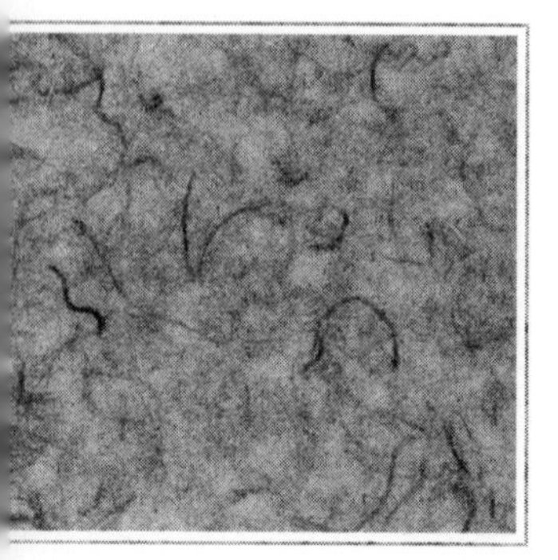

Some cooking methods

Baste	Moisten with gravy or melted fat/butter during cooking.
Bind	Add egg or melted fat or flour to dry ingredients in order to combine them.
Blanch	Immerse briefly in boiling water to ease the removal of skin like for almonds or tomatoes.
Broil	Roast/lightly fry. Also a term used for cooking meat.
Deep-frying	Fry in a lot of oil/ghee.
Fermentation	Effervescence caused by enzymes. Usually yeast is added to bread dough in order to raise it. Some batters, like that of *dosa* or *idli*, are kept overnight to ferment
Marinate	Soak meat, fish, etc., in a mixture of oil, spices or yogurt, before cooking.
Parboil	To simmer or boil till partially cooked.
Poach	To cook in liquid just below simmering point. Usually used for delicate foods that break if cooked at high heat.

Pot-roast	Method used for large pieces of meat, first browned and then cooked covered in very little liquid.
Pressure cooking	Food cooked under pressure. Higher the pressure, higher is the temperature at which the water boils. This way the food gets cooked faster since the steam created by the pressure is sealed in.
Puree	Make a soft pulp of vegetables or fruit and reduce to a smooth paste.
Refresh	To cool hot food quickly either under running water or by dipping in ice cold water to stop the cooking.
Roast	Heat/lightly fry, before grinding in case of spices. Cook in an oven.
Sauté	Quickly fry in a little hot oil.
Sift	To shake a dry, powdered substance through a sieve to remove any lumps or impurities and to add lightness.
Simmer	To cook gently in liquid that bubbles steadily just below boiling point. This way the food gets cooked evenly without breaking up.
Skim	To remove the surface layer of liquid, often impurities or scum, with a spoon.
Stew	To simmer a variety of vegetables or meat and spices in sufficient liquid.
Stir-fry	To cook small pieces of food in a little fat on heat stirring constantly.
Temper	*Tadka*, *baghar*. The first step in certain recipes : Heat oil. Add mustard seeds/cumin seeds to it. After they crackle, add the other spices/curry leaves.

I'm enclosing Cheque/DD No. ________________ dated ________________ for Rs. ____________ (in words) ______________________________ on (specify bank and branch) ______________________________

favouring **Popular Prakashan Pvt Ltd, Mumbai**

For Credit Cards

Charge Card ☐ VISA ☐ Master Card for Rs. ________________

Credit Card No. ☐☐☐☐☐☐☐☐☐☐☐☐☐☐☐☐

Card Expiry Date ☐☐ ☐☐ Card Member's Date Birth ☐☐ ☐☐ ☐☐☐☐

MM YY DD MM YYYY

Card Member's Name ______________________________

For ☐ Yellow Chilli Subscription ☐ Red Chilli Subscription

Name: Mr./Ms ______________________________

Address: ______________________________

____

City: ____________ Pin: ____________ State: ____________

Country: ________________ Phone Res.: ________________

Off.: ____________ E-mail: ________________

Please fill in the coupon in capital letters and mail it with your Cheque/DD to :

Popular Prakashan Pvt Ltd,
35-C, Pt. Madan Mohan Malaviya Marg,
Tardeo, Mumbai - 400 034.
Phone : 022-24941656, 24944295
Fax : 022-24945294
E-mail : info@popularprakashan.com
Website : www.popularprakashan.com

*Delivery subject to realisation of Cheque/DD.
Please allow two weeks for processing your subscription. Please superscribe your name and address on the reverse of the Cheque/DD.
All disputes are subject to the exclusive jurisdiction of competent courts and forums in Mumbai (India) only.

TERMS AND CONDITIONS FOR REDEMPTION

1. This coupon can be redeemed against the purchase of Sanjeev Kapoor books by sending this coupon along with payment to Popular Prakashan.
2. The offer is valid as per the mentioned date.
3. The coupons are valid only against the printed MRPs and will not work with any other special offers or promotions at the time of purchase.
4. The coupons are non-transferable and non-encashable.
5. No two vouchers can be clubbed together.
6. Each coupon is valid for one time purchase only.

Popular Prakashan Pvt. Ltd.
35-C, Pt. Madan Mohan Malaviya Marg, Tardeo,
Mumbai-400 034
E-Mail: info@popularprakashan.com
Phone: 91-22-24941656 Fax: 91-22-24945294

TERMS AND CONDITIONS FOR REDEMPTION

1. This coupon can be redeemed against the purchase of Sanjeev Kapoor books by sending this coupon along with payment to Popular Prakashan.
2. The offer is valid as per the mentioned date.
3. The coupons are valid only against the printed MRPs and will not work with any other special offers or promotions at the time of purchase.
4. The coupons are non-transferable and non-encashable.
5. No two vouchers can be clubbed together.
6. Each coupon is valid for one time purchase only.

Popular Prakashan Pvt. Ltd.
35-C, Pt. Madan Mohan Malaviya Marg, Tardeo,
Mumbai-400 034
E-Mail: info@popularprakashan.com
Phone: 91-22-24941656 Fax: 91-22-24945294

TERMS AND CONDITIONS FOR REDEMPTION

1. This coupon can be redeemed against the purchase of Sanjeev Kapoor books by sending this coupon along with payment to Popular Prakashan.
2. The offer is valid as per the mentioned date.
3. The coupons are valid only against the printed MRPs and will not work with any other special offers or promotions at the time of purchase.
4. The coupons are non-transferable and non-encashable.
5. No two vouchers can be clubbed together.
6. Each coupon is valid for one time purchase only.

Popular Prakashan Pvt. Ltd.
35-C, Pt. Madan Mohan Malaviya Marg, Tardeo,
Mumbai-400 034
E-Mail: info@popularprakashan.com
Phone: 91-22-24941656 Fax: 91-22-24945294

TERMS AND CONDITIONS FOR REDEMPTION

1. This coupon can be redeemed against the purchase of Sanjeev Kapoor books by sending this coupon along with payment to Popular Prakashan.
2. The offer is valid as per the mentioned date.
3. The coupons are valid only against the printed MRPs and will not work with any other special offers or promotions at the time of purchase.
4. The coupons are non-transferable and non-encashable.
5. No two vouchers can be clubbed together.
6. Each coupon is valid for one time purchase only.

Popular Prakashan Pvt. Ltd.
35-C, Pt. Madan Mohan Malaviya Marg, Tardeo,
Mumbai-400 034
E-Mail: info@popularprakashan.com
Phone: 91-22-24941656 Fax: 91-22-24945294